Miss Uniontown 1951:

NO REGRETS?

NO REGRETS!

Miss Uniontown 1951:

NO REGRETS?

—❧❧—

NO REGRETS!

A compelling and deeply moving
memoir from the 1950's

PLUS CONTEEN HALL

Published by Advantage, Charleston, South Carolina.
Member of Advantage Media Group.

Cover Photo: Paulette Mertes Studios, West Hartford, Ct.

ADVANTAGE is a registered trademark and the Advantage colophon is a trademark of Advantage Media Group, Inc.

Printed in the United States of America.

ISBN: 978-1-59932-265-0
LCCN: 2011911283

This publication is designed to provide accurate and authoritative information in regard to the subject matter covered. It is sold with the understanding that the publisher is not engaged in rendering legal, accounting, or other professional services. If legal advice or other expert assistance is required, the services of a competent professional person should be sought.

Advantage Media Group is proud to be a part of the Tree Neutral® program. Tree Neutral offsets the number of trees consumed in the production and printing of this book by taking proactive steps such as planting trees in direct proportion to the number of trees used to print books. To learn more about Tree Neutral, please visit www.treeneutral.com. To learn more about Advantage's commitment to being a responsible steward of the environment, please visit www.advantagefamily.com/green

Advantage Media Group is a leading publisher of business, motivation, and self-help authors. Do you have a manuscript or book idea that you would like to have considered for publication? Please visit www.amgbook.com or call 1.866.775.1696

Dedication

In memory of my husband Frank M. Hall, MD
for 47 years of Love and Laughter. Thank you to my three lovely
daughters, Susan Hall Lynch, Kelly Hall Urich and Kerry L. Hall
for your support, encouragement, enthusiasm and Love.

Acknowledgements

Thank You to the Advantage Media Publishing Team.
Much appreciation to Alison Morse, Kim Hall and my editor,
Brooke White. You believed in me, and made the
writing adventure interesting and fun.

Thank you to my God-daughter Lori Bove Campana
and her husband, Bob.

Plus

Table of Contents

Chapter One

***

MISS UNIONTOWN

CHAPTER ONE: MISS UNIONTOWN

New Year's Day 1950

*W*hat a great New Year's Eve I had! My seven best friends, one being my steady, had dinner at my house. Then we were on to the next house to dance and welcome in the New Year and the new decade. My curfew was 1:00 A.M., and I made it. I was a junior in high school and having a great time.

My New Year's wish for the '50s and my life was that this decade would continue to be happy and healthy, and that my big dream – to be accepted at Allegheny General Hospital School of Nursing in Pittsburgh – would come true. On this day, I decided to start a journal, because this was going to be my decade. Little did I know what an exciting decade it would be, but there are always some unexpected things that stop it from being perfect. The winter was the usual, cold and snowy. My friends and I walked wherever we went, cold or not. Basketball season was a big deal then, and I loved movies too. The malt shop hang-out was the Campus Dairy Bar, where the juke box played continuously and my feet never stopped dancing from the minute I walked in 'till I walked out. This fabulous spot was next door to the high school, and we often had lunch there, or would run over for a Coke between classes or after school. It was such a special, happy place.

Ready for Some Fancy Stepping

UNIONTOWN CUTIES—In their Summer and Fall appearances this year, the Uniontown American Legion Drum and Bugle Corps will be paced by a bevy of majorettes. Shown just after their first appearance above, are from the left, Peggy Lloyd, Marlene Colbert, Placida Conteen, Patsy Thompson, Joyce Struble and Janet Devan.

The Majorettes make the Pittsburgh-Post Gazette.

My happy cheerleading days. That's me on the right at the end.

The Summer of 1950

It was a fun summer. I had a part-time job at Montgomery Ward department store, where I was a sales clerk and did some junior modeling. I was a majorette for the Uniontown American Legion band and marched in the summer parades and special events, there and in Pittsburgh and surrounding areas.

Uniontown is a city in Fayette County, western Pennsylvania, 50 miles southeast of Pittsburgh and part of the Pittsburgh Metro Area. It is the county seat and largest city of Fayette County.

To the people coming over the last ridge of the Alleghenies over 200 years ago, the view of our valley must have been one of surpassing beauty. As far as the eye could see, there would have been the carpet of trees undisturbed through the centuries, extending westward to the gently rising hills, which border the Monongahela River.

"The Town of Union" was named by Henry Beeson on July 4, 1776, the same date as the United States Declaration of Independence (the timing was coincidental).

A Mr. Taylor of Dawson found how to produce coke, and it was found under our town. In the few miles up and down our valley, there lay a bed of what was called the Connellsville coking coal—the best in the world for making steel.

People hurried to try to buy "coal land" and tracts became very valuable so that at one time Uniontown was said to have more millionaires per capital than any town in the United States.

Reference: History of Uniontown by Miss Jean Brownfield.

My boyfriend at the time was a really great guy named Earl. He was getting ready to leave for Penn State College with two of his best friends, Weeg and Joey, part of our close-knit high school group at North Union.

Earl and I started going steady the last part of my sophomore year into my junior year. He was a football player and I was a cheerleader – perfect, right? Well, almost, but we foolishly seemed to argue a lot over nothing. By the time he left for Penn State we had broken up, but remained very good friends for years.

Senior Year, 1951

September of 1950 started my senior year. If I could pass my chemistry class and the entrance exam at Pittsburgh University, I'd be entering Allegheny General Hospital next September in their three-year nursing program. I had wanted to be a nurse since I was seven years old, and had been dressed up as a Red Cross nurse on a float in the May Day Parade.

The football games were so much fun for us cheerleaders. We did flips, splits, high kicks, and higher jumps. The last game of the football season made me sad. I had been a cheerleader since basketball season of my freshman year, and I felt so fortunate to have been chosen that young. The magic was in being outdoors; running up and down the field, getting everyone cheering even when we were losing.

I passed Chemistry with a B-, and was chosen to be Lady in Waiting to the Spring Dance Queen. My Senior Prom was exactly what every teenager dreamed about; handsome date, beautiful white gown, gardenia wrist corsage. I double-dated with my best friends, Tish and Eddie, at the Country Club. Perfect!

Graduation Day was a very happy day. The ceremony was on the stage of the State Theater; one hundred and forty-four graduates all ready to party that night. My classmate Pat and I were excited for our coming adventure in September.

The Beauty Pageant, 1951

In the late spring of 1951, some gentlemen from the Lions Club called and spoke to my mother. With her permission, they wanted to invite me to enter the Miss Uniontown beauty contest. The winner would go on to compete for Miss Pennsylvania in Harrisburg, then on to Atlantic City for Miss America.

My mom had won Miss Uniontown in 1928, but she was very beautiful. I was cute, but certainly not beautiful.

I did have some talent. I had taken tap lessons off and on from the age of six, and also some ballet. A couple of the other dancing cheerleaders and I would perform at dances and different events, and sometimes entertain the residents at rest homes. I enjoyed entertaining.

Mom and I said "yes" to the Lions Club. Before starting to work hard for the contest we took ten days in early June to go visit our cousins in New York City, my graduation gift from Mom. I fell in love with Manhattan and Broadway. I didn't know then how important a part this city would play in my life.

On our return home, I went to work on my dancing and my walk, and practiced being interviewed. My mother lay down the law;

no more fries, cheeseburgers, or, heaven forbid, my favorite malt milkshakes. Oh boy! What had I gotten into?

The contest was held at Uniontown High School Stadium because it was very big. There were nine contestants. I thought one of the girls was really pretty and I'd probably end as runner-up.

My dance number went well, and after that I wasn't nervous anymore. The gown and bathing suit competition were fine, too. My question from the judges was, "What woman do you admire the most in history and why?" I'm sure you can guess my answer – that's right, Florence Nightingale.

When the MC announced the winner, and I heard my name, the newspapers said that I sat there for a moment, with my mouth open in shock. Then my "grace and poise" returned and I ran to the microphone. They also said the stadium erupted into such a roar of applause that you would have thought it was a touchdown.

The next morning as I was sitting in my dentist's chair, the radio announcer was talking about the new Miss Uniontown, Placeda Dee Conteen. I swear, Dr. P was so surprised that he almost dropped the drill! He and the staff couldn't believe that I had kept the appointment.

The next three weeks were so busy; lots of practice and hard work, because the stakes were higher now that I was in the running for Miss Pennsylvania. I was making public appearances and modeling, many pictures being taken, and of all things, fan mail started arriving for me. I was thrilled, and answered every letter.

On August 6, 1951 the newspapers, *The Morning Herald* and *The Evening Standard*, both featured articles sending me off to Harrisburg with many best wishes. We had quite a few friends and local folks who'd be traveling to Harrisburg to support me.

I was told to wear the Miss Uniontown banner when I arrived at the Penn Harris Hotel, so that I could be more easily identified for the extra hospitality arranged for the seventeen girls entered in the state competition.

Harry Daniels, manager of the State Theater in Harrisburg where the pageant was to be held that coming Wednesday evening, informed me all the contestants were scheduled to be guests on two radio programs, and to do an appearance at an army base Tuesday night. A rehearsal would be held at 1:30 Wednesday afternoon by Larry Woodin, the Western Pennsylvania Miss America director, who would act as master of ceremonies.

I was usually very calm and not easily intimidated. But when my name was called and I walked out on the stage in my beautiful, white, sparkling strapless gown, I absolutely froze for a few minutes. At first, I couldn't even smile.

When I went backstage to change, many of the photographers snapping my picture reassured me, saying that I'd done fine and that I had a good chance of winning. They were trying to make me relax and laugh, and it worked. I scored high in the bathing suit and gown competitions.

I knew my talent was somewhat weak, compared to some of the others'. I was also only 5'4" and the trend was starting to appreciate the taller girls. I don't even remember the judges' question!

I placed 3rd, 2nd runner up to Miss Pennsylvania. I had won a scholarship and prizes, and was happy just to have had the exciting experience. As it was explained to me, I had won 3rd place over approximately 270 girls, the number who'd entered the contest throughout the state.

The long ride back to Uniontown with Mom, my cousins, and boyfriend was not somber. Sure, we were disappointed, but we did have some laughs.

In less than a month I was on my way to becoming a nurse. I had wanted this since I was a little girl. I continued to do appearances and modeling until I left. My friends were calling me "The Golden Girl."

My mother gave me a going-away party. A classmate of mine, Pat, was going with me. A photographer and reporter were at the house taking pictures, and the front pages of the two local newspapers featured articles about it the next day.

Junior Modeling.

The Evening Standard

"THE PAPER THAT GOES INTO THE HOME"

UNIONTOWN, PENNSYLVANIA, THURSDAY, JULY 19, 1951

Here's Miss Uniontown

PLACEDA DEE CONTEEN

Placeda Dee Conteen New Miss Uniontown

So very happy!

graduated from North Union high

(See pictures on page 14)

school this year. She's now working part-time at the Montgomery Ward store and plans to enter purses' training in the fall.

Mother Won In 1928

And it's a case of like mother, like daughter.

Placeda Dee's mother, Vera McCall then and a resident of Youngstown, near Lemont, was Miss Uniontown of 1928.

The new Miss Uniontown's first reaction to the announcement that she had won was a delighted, open-mouthed stare. She quickly recovered, however, and received her awards with as much aplomb as she had shown in the "personality" quiz, although owning up she was a bit "shaky."

But the same applied to her mother. "I could hardly get down those steps," said Mrs. Conteen.

In the talent competition, Placeda Dee showed a strapless white organdy evening gown dotted with flashing sequins, which she had designed and made herself, and did a pert little tap-dance.

Tall, blond Patty Lou Swaney, daughter of Mr. and Mrs. Andrew J. Swaney of 420 Clarendon avenue, provided the feature of the evening in the talent contest, as well as drawing heavy applause

(Continued on Page 2, Col. 2)

"O. K."

New Miss Uniontown.

Placeda Dee Conteen it is, and you know something? She's pretty as a picture.

And the Lions club beauty pageant divertissement last night just as enjoyable as usual and a better night couldn't have been chosen, no sir, not with full ol' Mistah Moon hanging out of the skies and smiling all over the pretty gals.

Straight From The Notebook

Talk about the California gold strike and the 49ers!

They had something like that right here in Uniontown a few days ago.

A huge pile of ancient silver and gold coins, dating as far back as 1872, was found in the debris turned up when they dug out an underground gasoline storage tank at the William Salitrik Richfield station at the corner of West Fayette and Market streets (just west of Morgantown street).

"Buzz" Storey

Somebody estimated the value of the "find" at between $200 and $300 — anyhow, there were a lot of coins in that heap of dirt.

The odd part of it is that nobody knows for sure just how much "buried treasure" there was. Passersby evidently noticed the coins glittering in the dirt before the service station people themselves did—and promptly picked up a souvenir or two.

Salitrik's station was in the news earlier this week when gasoline fumes from the same hole ignited and burned three men.

Politics being politics, we couldn't get by without slogans.

Milton V. Munk, the Connellsville funeral director, who's unopposed for the Republican nomination as coroner, says he's "The Last Man to Let You Down."

And Jim Luckey, another Connellsville man, running for county commissioner on the GOP side of the fence, isn't a man to pass up the obvious. He has signs plastered on cars, "Be Happy—Vote Luckey."

County Controller John R. Hoye, a Democrat, who's aiming on going right back into that office, says his watchword is "One Good Term Deserves Another."

Add to the list of small industries in Fayette county the Ever-Flex Manufacturing company of Hopwood.

It's operated by Max E. Girz, a chemist with 35 years' experience in several companies, who was educated at the famous Heidelberg university in Germany. Mr. Girz just recently moved to Hopwood.

He makes "Film-Glo," a plastic-type film for chrome and auto finishes (it's not a wax; the car must be clean before it's applied), "Air-olite," a plastic cement, and "Klenz," a cleaner for car finishes.

Well, it was a good show and there were so many pretty girls around . . . Not only onstage, but in the stands, too. It's no wonder that Uniontown has the reputation from coast to coast of having the best-looking girls in the country (and this isn't Chamber-of-Commerce variety of local patriotism, either—ask any traveler.)

We're talking about that Miss Uniontown contest, of course—although from the cheers at the end you'd have thought somebody made a touchdown.

All kidding aside, the Lions Club did another fine job—and Miss Placeda Dee Conteen, as beautiful a young lady as ever wore that Miss Uniontown streamer, deserves all kinds of congratulations.

And Mr. Bill Means, the principal of North Union high school, had that proud-to-bursting smile on his face again—that's the fourth time in five years that a North Union girl has won the Miss Uniontown title: Betty Watt, 1947; Bernadine Benko, 1949; Dolores Folando, 1950, and now Miss Conteen.

Not to mention Mr. Bob Ware, the Montgomery Ward manager, Placeda Dee is working there during the summer—and Lil Hanford (now Mrs. Don Sneddon) who placed so high at Atlantic City four years ago, also was a Ward employe.

Larry Woodin, the emcee, enjoyed his usual jousting with the trains—the whistles won every time, and the proceedings had to stop until the trains went by.

Next on the agenda: taking Harrisburg by storm.

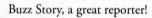

Buzz Story, a great reporter!

The Evening New

HARRISBURG, PENNA., THURSDAY, AUGUST 9, 195

BEAUTY, BEAUTY AND MORE BEAUTY—Statuesque Barbara Guff, left, Miss Greater Harrisburg, receives waves of applause as she walks in the evening gown competition in the Miss Pennsylvania contest in Harrisburg last night. But she didn't make the finals. Five other beauties did. They're shown above just before judges announced their choice. They are, from left: Louise Simmons, Miss Greater Johnstown; Clare Lippert, Miss Kiski Valley; Margaret Hudy, Miss Greater Lehigh Valley; Elizabeth Redcay, Miss North Central Pennsylvania; and Placeda Dee Conteen, Miss Uniontown. And the winner and Miss Pennsylvania 1952—vivacious Clare Lippert—gets a congratulatory hug from mother. She'll go to the Atlantic City Miss America Pageant to represent the state.

In the Top 5! I'm on the far right.

MISS UNIONTOWN PREPARES FOR STATE ELIMINATIONS

(Continued From Page One)

"We are so happy up here, we would like to close the store and celebrate."

The popular girl is receiving congratulations from friends and casual acquaintances—all rejoicing over the honor that is hers and proud to have her represent the city in the state eliminations August 8 in Harrisburg.

Applause showed the large audience approved of the selection made by the judges at the pageant. Placeda was a vision of loveliness as she gracefully glided across the stage in a size 9 white strapless lace net evening gown—the bouffant skirt emphasizing her 24-inch waistline. Her beautiful teeth flashed as she smiled self-assured-ly.

Top Dance

Miss Uniontown Is Third In State Beauty Contest

"Miss Uniontown," Placeda Dee Conteen, won third place in the state beauty pageant finals last night at Harrisburg.

Winner of the Miss Pennsylvania title was Clara Marie Lippart of Tarentown, a tall brunette singer who was in the state competition as Miss Kiski Valley. She'll represent Pennsylvania in the Miss America finals at Atlantic City.

"Miss Uniontown," Placeda Dee Conteen. The second-place winner was the Elizabeth Redray, of Selingsrove, a tall blond whose talent was modeling. She was Miss North Central Pennsylvania.

Placeda Dee, whose talent was dancing, had been crowned Miss Uniontown at the Lions Club beauty pageant here last month. Lions President Dick Spellman, who went to Harrisburg for the state competition, said, "We were

proud of her. Placeda's stage presence and poise were outstanding—the crowd was with her from the start.

"She 'knocked 'em dead' in both bathing and evening gown and up to the last minute we thought she had the crown. But the competition was very stiff, particularly in talent."

The 18-year-old local girl was accompanied to Harrisburg by her mother, Mrs. Vera Conteen. The $250 scholarship she won in the Uniontown show will go toward her nurses' training at Allegheny General hospital, where she plans to enroll in a few weeks.

Evening Star
"THE PAPER THAT GOES INTO THE HOME"
UNIONTOWN, PENNSYLVANIA, THURSDAY, AUGUST 9, 1951

Miss Uniontown Places Third

—Evening Standard Photo
Placeda Dee Conteen, above, carried Uniontown's banner into the state beauty-pageant finals at Harrisburg last night and placed third in a field of 16 girls. See story on page 28.

The swimsuit shot. Pleased to have placed.

—Evening Standard Photo

Placeda Dee Conteen, right above, prepares to open the gifts at a farewell party last night. With her are her mother, Mrs. Vera Conteen, center, and Patty Guesman. Miss Conteen and Miss Guesman will enter Allegheny General hospital School of Nursing on Monday.

Miss Uniontown '51 In Nurses Training

Placeda Dee Conteen To Apply Scholarship
Award To Good Use; To Train At Allegheny

Blond and beautiful Placeda Dee Conteen, Miss Uniontown of 1951, leaves Monday for nurses' training at Allegheny General hospital, Pittsburgh.

That's where she'll apply the $250 scholarship presented to her when she won the Miss Uniontown title at the Lions Club beauty pageant in July.

Miss Conteen went on from here to place third in the state beauty contest finals at Harrisburg.

Also leaving for the Pittsburgh hospital's School of Nursing, along with Placeda, will be Patty Guesman.

Placeda, daughter of Mrs. Vera Conteen, was given a farewell party last night at her home, 120 East Main street.

Present at the affair were Mrs. Leoda Bryson and daughters, Frances and Shirley; Mrs. Rose Somarada and daughter, Roseann; Dolores Amandola, Tisse Dodson, Dolly Raisbeck, Betty Jean Minerd, Mrs. Betty Minerd, Patty Guesman, Martha Lavoty, Bernadine Trocheck, Mrs. Vera Conteen, the hostess, and the guest of honor, Placeda Dee Conteen.

"O. K."

Chapter Two

NURSE IN TRAINING

CHAPTER 2: NURSE IN TRAINING

The Residence: September 1951

*S*eptember 1951 was here, and I was all packed and ready for a new adventure. Our mothers were driving us to Pittsburgh.

When you walked into the Nurses' Residence, there was a large desk facing you. Twenty-four hours a day, this was where the house mothers signed you out and in. On it was phones, intercom, and a typewriter. It looked like a hotel lobby.

There were many small living rooms off the long hall that was on each side of the main lobby. At the end of the east hall was a large living room with couches, comfortable chairs, T.V., a radio, and a desk; very pretty and homey.

Also off the main lobby were two elevators and a handsome circular staircase going down. The second floor had large and small classrooms, labs, and offices. Other classrooms were in the hospital.

Every floor had a large living room facing you as you stepped off the elevator. There was a phone booth on each floor, which had a pay phone and house phone, and a large communal bathroom on each end. The small kitchen wasn't used much, as we took our meals in our own dining room at the hospital.

The rooms were attractive, mostly doubles, higher up, with some singles. Since we had maid service, all we had to do was to make our beds.

My new roommate, Myrna, was a delight. Despite our very different personalities, we got along wonderfully. There were one hundred girls starting a new adventure on this day.

Our uniforms were a grey/blue shift with a stiff white collar and short sleeves with starched cuffs, a large black scarf tied in a bow, and a starched white half-apron that buttoned in the back. This was our probie uniform for the first six months. The worst part of this already hideous outfit was the black shoes and stockings. Not exactly in keeping with the picture I'd had of myself as the Angel of Mercy in glowing white!

My third or fourth week I received a phone call from the nursing administers office, setting up an appointment for me with Miss C. I couldn't figure out why; I asked if any of the other girls had gotten that call. They hadn't. I was ushered into the inner sanctum and after a few cold pleasantries, I was offered a seat.

Miss C. got to the point. I would not be regarded here as Miss Uniontown Beauty Queen. I wonder how she knew about the title, and then remembered it had been in the Pittsburgh papers. She instructed me to get rid of the peroxide streak I had in my naturally medium blond hair, and to leave it natural from now on. I was crushed – nobody had ever verbally attacked me like that before. I wasn't even sure what I'd done wrong. When I got back to my room, I tossed out the peroxide.

I should have been an A student, but I was barely making Bs in high school – I was just having too much fun. I literally had to learn how to study, I had no time for dates and that was fine, but many evenings the girls would just go for walks or ice cream and I couldn't go. In our main courses – Anatomy, Biology, Chemistry, and Pharmacology – we had to keep a C+ average, and I struggled, determined to make good in this profession I'd always wanted.

After the first 6 months, there was a capping ceremony in our residence in the auditorium for family and a few friends. We received the bib which attached to our white apron, and our white caps. It was a great thrill, even though we were stuck with the damn black shoes and stockings until graduation.

After six months, our probation period was over and we were now working all shifts, days and nights, never getting off on time. If we were on days, we had to go to chapel in the auditorium before breakfast, and if you were late, you lost your going home privileges. We worked double-time, carrying our long shifts while also taking full-time classes and studying. Our weekends, when we got them off, started at noon on Saturday and you had to be back by 10 on Sunday night. Complain? Yes, we certainly did, but it was the best, most satisfying, interesting, emotional, tiring, rewarding work I could imagine, and I loved it!

That year at the big May Day Parade in Uniontown, I was sitting on the back of a Cadillac convertible, wearing a beautiful black and gold gown. I still had the crown until July; the title, forever. I crowned the New Miss Uniontown in July.

The second big event that spring was the wedding of my best friend and fellow cheerleader, Tish, to the love of her life, Eddie. I was the maid of honor. What a great day!

My junior year I was dating an intern occasionally. We were both big Pittsburgh Pirate fans and went to as many games as we could. Sometimes he would get lucky and an attending physician or a patient would give him tickets to the game. In the medical world, the lowest ones on the food chain were the student nurses, followed by the interns, so we tended to stick together.

Don't you love the outfits?

My mom got remarried May 30, 1953, to a wonderful man who was crazy about her. It was a big wedding -- fifteen of my friends came with their dates. I had been dating a really nice young man, Jerry, who was in the insurance business. His folks owned a couple of Dairy Bar Restaurants in Troy Hill -- great sandwiches, ice cream, a juke box. Some evenings and weekends when he worked, my girlfriends and I would help, singing and dancing as we served the customers. What fun everyone had!

Jerry was one of the funniest, sweetest fellas I had ever dated. He could sing, dance, he was loved by all, and was also handsome. We all had a great time at my mom's wedding.

September of 1953 we started our senior year. At last we were seniors, with a few more privileges -- and I do mean a few!

Freddie's Death: October 1953

One morning when I came on duty at 10:00, I was told that an emergency case had just arrived by ambulance and the family was asking for me. I looked up and saw my Aunt Margaret standing there. Her husband Freddie was just being examined by the doctors. I ran into the room to see what was happening. His speech was slurred, and he had partial paralyses of the left side of his face, but the doctors didn't think it was a stroke. Freddie was 28 years old, my aunt 26 years old and their daughter Sharon nearly 2.

Freddie was on my floor for about 10 days, so we spent a lot of time together. He knew me, and we would talk, but he was hard to understand. I would shave him every other day, and come back after my shift was over to read to him.

Days passed and still there was not a diagnosis. I was getting frustrated, but I couldn't say anything; I was only a student. It was decided that he would be moved to a veteran's hospital.

A week and a half later, he died. His was the first death in my mom's family and deeply affected all of us.

Freddie's funeral was on a beautiful sunny Sunday afternoon in October, with a procession of at least one hundred cars to the cemetery. As I looked out the back window of the limo, I was overwhelmed watching car after car, as far as you could see, coming over the lush, autumn-colored hills. I will always remember that sad day. His autopsy said that he had died of a brain abscess.

Seniors: Psychiatric Training, 1954

As seniors, we did our psychiatric training for 13 weeks at Warren State, in Warren, Pennsylvania. The grounds and buildings were beautiful, like a big college campus. Passing by, you would never guess that it housed the mentally ill, including the criminally insane. The mornings when we were on shower duty, we wore the same dresses as the patients. The only difference was the chains we wore around our waists with lots of keys hanging off. We walked right into the shower with our clothes on. Some of the patients didn't want to go in the shower, and they would call us the Allegheny bitches. One of the hardest things I had to do was prepare the patients, male and female, for their electric shock treatments. They cried and begged us not to take them into the room. We had to strap them to the table. Sometimes we stayed with them, other times we walked out and watched the treatment through a big window, then went back in and wheeled them out. Their fear and the brutality of the procedure troubled me, and I've never forgotten it.

We had day room duty, at times with almost a hundred patients in a large room, and we'd try to interest them in games. This is where I learned to play pinochle, although I was never sure if I knew how to play, since the rules would change from day to day depending on who you were playing with.

Two nurses would walk together around and around this gigantic room. If a lot of the patients were more agitated than usual on a given day, we would walk with one nurse walking forward and the partner nurse walking backwards, switching occasionally.

On cafeteria duty one dinnertime, my friend Jo got hurt. The patients had sectioned metal trays and waited in a moving line. This dinnertime, she stepped in to prevent a patient from cutting to the head of the line, which would have caused a riot. My line was next to hers and I watched as this man lifted his tray. I started to yell, "Jo, look out!" but it was too late. She went down, fortunately only dazed, not out.

I think a lot of us grew up very fast on this rotation. We learned so much; we were frightened at times, but what an experience.

I spent Thanksgiving there, went home for Christmas, then back for New Year's. Our group left at the end of February.

We still had housemothers and signed out and in, but the hours and our rules were a little more flexible. Girls came from different hospitals throughout Pennsylvania.

By the time I went home, I had gained 12 pounds. The food was delicious, mostly prepared by the patients. I can still taste those homemade donuts.

We returned back to A.G.H. in time to have our graduation pictures taken for the yearbook. I didn't know this was going to happen, and I had just cut my hair myself. It was way too short. With my chopped hair and chubby cheeks I was a real "vision in white."

My senior vacation was the first two weeks in March. They were very uneventful, but Jerry was happy I was back in Pittsburgh. It was quite a change. Not as much freedom, and we missed our new friends. Seven months to the big day. Would I ever get there?

Chapter Three

THE CREW-CUTS

CHAPTER 3: THE CREW-CUTS

The Record: Crazy 'Bout Ya Baby

*I*t was early spring, 1954. It seemed like every time I turned on the radio, I'd hear this song "Crazy 'Bout Ya Baby" by the Crew-Cuts. Now, I had seen the 4 Aces and they were terrific, listened to the Four Lads and The Four Freshman, and I'd never heard of the Crew-Cuts. But this song was so catchy, and the harmony was great. I'd turn the radio up every time it came on, and sing along – not well at all, but that didn't stop me. Any time it came on the radio, all the girls on my floor would yell, "Plus (my nickname), they're playing your song!"

On Saturday, the day before Easter, I was off by noon, on a street car to downtown Pittsburgh. I was walking to the bus station to go home to Uniontown for the holiday. As I walked past a record store, my song was playing, and there in the window was a big picture of four good-looking guys with matching crew cuts smiling back at me. I went right in and blew my bus fare to buy the record. Luckily, I still had tokens left for the streetcar, so I retraced my steps and returned to the residence. My roommate Les was just coming off duty and was surprised to see me sitting at the desk.

"Why aren't you home?" she wanted to know.

"I spent my fare on a record. Now I have to call my mother."

"Well, you can come home with me for the holiday or I can loan you the money," Les offered. Her folks lived about twenty minutes away in Troy Hill.

"I think the latter idea would sit better with my mother." I put the record in its jacket, stuck it in my suitcase, and got onto the next streetcar for the bus station, getting home a couple of hours later than expected.

I was getting off of the elevator back at the Nurses' Residence a few weeks later when I heard my friend Jo calling, "Plus, come quick, hurry!"

"What? I only have 10 minutes for a cigarette and back I go–"

Jo grabbed me and hustled me down to Mo's room. Ten girls were already in there, all of them quiet and listening intently to the disc jockey, Art Palen, saying that in two weeks the Crew-Cuts will be appearing at the Copa for a one week engagement and "now here are the Crew-Cuts, singing 'Sh-boom,'" and all of us sang along, every word of it.

As I walked to the elevator I turned and said, "I want you all to know I will be going to the Copa. I don't know how or what night, but I'm going."

Pat asked, "How are you going to get out of here? You have to sign in and out." Our training program was most rigid and autocratic.

I knew there had to be a way. "Everyone put on your thinking caps, and I'll see you later."

As far as I was concerned, the hard part was going to be figuring out what to wear. "Look, I have this great pair of black heels and my mother's pearls, all I need is a black dress." I remember Jo was wearing red, beautiful with her black hair. Jo and Mo are roommates along with Les, we're all best friends.

The girls scrambled for their closets, and four black dresses suddenly appeared, all my size! I'm trying to choose and it's not that easy, even with fifteen women weighing in with their opinions as I modeled. Finally, they all just took a vote. The plain black dress with the square neckline and long sleeves won. It was gorgeous!

Now, someone had to time how long it takes us to walk down eight flights of stairs, heels in hand. Exactly how many minutes would it take for two of you to get on the elevator, get off on the first floor, and distract our Housemother, Mrs. R? Timing was key.

The connector to the hospital was a long tunnel from the lower level in our building where the auditorium and the gym were located. The first floor of the hospital was at the end of the passageway. We had to get through the corridor, past the Urology Unit, the gift shop, elevators, the information desk, the lobby, and out the front door and into a cab, without being seen. Assuming we made it out, we'd have to do the whole thing over again in reverse to sneak back to our dorm.

"You're crazy to take the risk! It's only five months to gradua-tion. If you get caught, you'll be expelled," Pat kept saying. But I'm hard to talk out of something once I make my mind up, and I was determined to think positive. Otherwise, I knew I'd lose my nerve.

We worked the day shift on Wednesday, and by 7:30 that night, we were in a cab on our way to the Copa.

The Copa was a very exclusive, very swank supper club in downtown Pittsburgh. To our surprise, the maître d' ushered us to a ringside table. We sat, sipping pink ladies, trying to look as though we did this every night of the week.

Suddenly the lights went down, the band struck up those familiar chords, and the M.C. was saying, "Here they are, the 'Sh-Boom' boys, the Crew-Cuts!" There went Jo's and my little attempt at looking sophisticated - you couldn't have wiped the smiles from our faces. They could have sung "Mary Had a Little Lamb" and it would have been terrific! The show lasted just over an hour, and they were gone. Jo and I were trying to decide – should we stay for the next show or leave? It wasn't for two hours.

We had no curfew; we were staying the night at our graduate nurse friends' apartment in Troy Hill. They'd given us a key and said to pull down the Murphy bed in the living room; they'd see us in the A.M.

After discussing the fact that we did risk so much to be there, we decided that we would stay. I went to the ladies room. On the way, I spotted two Crew-Cuts, Rudi and Ray, sitting at a table near the bar.

They both started to get up, but Rudi got up immediately, walked over to me and said, "Did you enjoy the show?"

"It was great, especially my favorite, 'Crazy 'Bout Ya Baby,' also 'Sh-Boom' and 'World on a String,' and you did a great job with 'Pretend.'" I stopped, and said "You asked me one question and I gave you ten answers," thinking, oh, boy, back up, but he was laughing. I took a deep breath, "Yes, we enjoyed the show very much."

"Are you staying for the next show?"

We were trying to decide. He said, "We have to visit a few disc jockeys. Would you and your friend go with us and then come back for the second show? While I go to the powder room, why don't you ask her? I'm Rudi."

"I know. She is Jo and I am Plus."

"You will have to explain that name to me later."

Jo was agreeable to the plan. We waited in the lobbies of the radio stations as the Crew Cuts were interviewed. We ran from one station to another.

We went back to the club, with plans to get a bite to eat after the show. Johnnie made the fourth person. Of course, we told them that we were already RN's, with our own apartments.

Rudi asked if we would care to come back before their engagement was over. I said "Yes," but explained that tomorrow, or rather today, we were working the evening shift and it was too late to change it.

"I'll call you tomorrow. What time do you leave for work?" he asked.

"I am out the door at 2:10 P.M."

"We are booked all morning, but I will call before you go to work."

It was 2:30 A.M. as we got out of the cab in front of the apartment. He kissed me goodnight. I was happy, but I can't say that I believed he would call me. I could just hope.

The girls had looked out the window when they heard voices, saw the kiss, and wanted to hear about the whole evening. One of the roommates slept through the whole event and was upset to think she missed the kiss.

Our guardian angels were with us. We got back into the residence the same way we'd gotten out. I have to say my heart was beating so fast I was having palpitations. I was now afraid we would be seen but, thank God, we made it! I promised myself I'd never try anything like this again.

The Call

Back in the dorms, ten girls were pacing up and down the hall. We were waiting to see if Rudi would call as he'd promised he would, before I went on duty. 2:10 came, but no call. I was disappointed, oh yes, but really not surprised. As I walked toward the elevator, the phone rang. One of the girls picked up before the ring was finished, and I ran back.

It was him! "I'm sorry; I just got out of a radio interview."

"Rudi, I can't talk now, I have to hurry – but call me when you get settled after your last show. I will be waiting at 12:45 A.M. And, Rudi?"

"Yes?"

"Thanks for the call."

We were not allowed to receive calls after 10 P.M., ever, even if it was an emergency, it would have to go through the house mother. At 12:30 A.M., I was in my nightgown, carrying a pillow and a light blanket. I snuck into the phone booth, and scrunched down on the floor to wait. At exactly 12:45, the phone rang. I grabbed it before it could wake anyone. We talked 'till 2 in the morning, making plans to go to dinner the next evening at 6.

We met outside a charming little Italian restaurant with red and white checkered tablecloths, and we walked in holding hands.

As our appetizers came, I couldn't eat. I put my fork down and said, "I have a confession to make. I can't get any of this delicious food down until I tell you something." He looked concerned. "I'm not a R.N. with an apartment; I'm a senior student nurse with almost five months before graduation. I live in the nurses' residence; I'm not the angel in white yet. I'm so sorry I lied, I just – why are you laughing, is that a happy laugh or an angry one?" I asked.

"I am so happy, that's all it is, I was afraid you were engaged or going steady. I'm so relieved." He took my hand and squeezed it.

I smiled and said, "Tell me about yourself, and start from when you were an adorable little boy."

We had to rush back to the Copa for the 8:30 show. Johnnie, Ray, and Pat kept me company as Rudi changed. They were sweet, polite, and funny. Could they get me a seat? I would be getting a cab at 9:15 (they still didn't know I had a ten o'clock curfew). I would stand in the back; I just wanted to hear my favorite song. At 9:15 I gave a little wave and walked out as "Sh-Boom" was ending to enthusiastic applause from the packed house. My Crew-Cuts were a big Pittsburgh HIT.

That night on the phone, Rudi told me that when I waved, turned and walked out without looking back, he had a sinking feeling I was walking out of his life, and he could hardly finish the show.

Saturday, we spent hours on the phone before my shift started. Between his disc jockey interviews and visiting record stores, I called on my half-hour dinner break; he called after I got off duty, and after his last show. Was I in a dream? I had never met a man that was so exciting and considerate. I was 21 and he was 23.

Sunday was a casual, fun day. We started with 9:30 Mass and breakfast. I showed him around my favorite city, and we took a walk in the park, rode the street car, and took the incline up to Mount Washington.

I came back to quickly change for dinner. I still had to be in by 10:00 P.M. Only on Saturdays, seniors had a pass until 11:00. So, back we went to our restaurant with the checkered tablecloths and the nice owner fawning over us.

That night, Rudi refused to say goodbye. They were leaving the next day for Rochester, NY. He came to say goodbye on Monday morning. I had a class, but as soon as it was over I ran all the way to the residence. He was waiting in the lobby. We went in one of the small living rooms and we kissed. He promised to call that night and to write the next day. He started to tell me he was falling in love with me, but I stopped him.

"No – don't say something you're not sure of, or that you might want to take back later. Let's talk about something else." Walking out of the living room, holding hands, he stopped to say goodbye to the house mother, who was flattered.

When we walked outside on the top step, he said he wasn't falling in love with me – he was in love with me! I put my fingers up to his lips to stop him, kissed him and said goodbye. As he walked down the steps to the waiting cab I called "Rudi, wait!" I ran down the steps and into his arms. "I love you, too, but please don't hurt me."

"I will never hurt you, I love you." We looked up and there were faces looking back at us from nearly every window. Rudy grinned, and yelled, "She loves me!"

Happy faces, one more kiss, and he was gone. I watched the cab 'till it was out of sight. Would I really see him again? This was only the sixth day since we'd met; was our love possible? The phone rang that night, and we could have talked forever!

RICHFORD HOTEL   ROCHESTER, N.Y.

ENJOY
THE FRIENDLY
COMFORTS
OF THE
RICHFORD

MODERN
FIREPROOF
ECONOMICAL

350 ROOMS

ELM & CHESTNUT STS.
HAMILTON 5500

May 10, 1951

My Dear Plac;

Well we just finished rehearsal and we were out late, we didn't get into Rochester till about 5:30, so we didn't rehearse till about seven.

I feel real lonely without you honey, and please believe me when I tell you that I love you so much, that it really hurts me to ever be away from you.

It's still hard to believe, because it happened so fast but I never was so sure of anything in all my life. I love you very much, and want you to be mine alway.

RICHFORD HOTEL ROCHESTER, N.Y.

ENJOY
THE FRIENDLY
COMFORTS
OF THE
RICHFORD

MODERN
FIREPROOF
ECONOMICAL

350 ROOMS

ELM & CHESTNUT STS.
HAMILTON 5500

②

I promise I'll be true to you always
and I'll never hurt you in any way, honor.
I've finally found you, and I never want to
lose you.

Honey take real good care of yourself
and remember that I'm thinking about you all
the time, and I'll sing "Pere" to-nite and
every nite just for you.

I'll be phoning you to-morrow and
I'll phone you again on Sunday at your home,
and don't forget at 1:00 o'clock every morning
we got to think real hard about each other, that
way we've got a special time to say we love each
other every day.

I'll close now, honey. I'll write

RICHFORD HOTEL   ROCHESTER, N.Y.

ENJOY
THE FRIENDLY
COMFORTS
OF THE
RICHFORD

MODERN
FIREPROOF
ECONOMICAL
—
350 ROOMS

ELM & CHESTNUT STS.

HAMILTON 5500

③

again to-morrow. With this letter I send all my love. If you write as soon as you get this letter. I'll be able to get your reply before I leave here. I'm at the Richford Hotel, Rm 605. I think it's better to send your reply here, then to the Triton where were playing at.

All My Love

Always & Forever

Rudi

P.S. Boo!

May 12, 1951
Rochester N. Y.

My Dearest Plac;

Hi, honey just a few more
lines to let you know that I'm thinking
about you all the time. I've got a few
minutes so I'd thought I'd write you to
prove to you that I meant everything that
I told you.

How is everything going with
you? Real great I hope! I don't like
the club here at all. Its real dead, after
the Copa, and the boss here is a real
funny guy. I just can't understand
him. I'll be glad when we get to Dayton
next week.

We've started to visit the disc
jockeys here, and in about 15 minutes

6

we've got to see another one. We're going to visit a lot of the record stores here too. The Record isn't as popular here as it is in Pittsburgh, but it's just starting to catch on, maybe by the time we leave here we can get it really moving.

We ll, honey thats all the news for now. Don't forget I'll phone you on Saturday about 6:30 at home, and I'll write again to-morrow. Thinking About You Always

All My Love - Always & Forever

Rudi

P.S. My address for next week will be the "Esquire Red Room Club" Dayton Ohio

don't forget to mention in C/O Crew-Cuts

Frid. May 12 - 52 3 30 P.M.

My Dearest Plus;

Honey, just received your latest
letter, the one on the blue stationery, and by
the way, I've received all your letters including
the ones you sent to the Triton.

Happy Anniversary to you to,
darling. I want you to know, Plus, that ever
since I've met you my whole life is
changed. I think of you from morning
till night. I wish there were more than
24 hrs a day, then there would be more time
for me to be saying I love you. I love
you so much that honestly, and (believe me
when I say this) I can't wait till the day
we can be married, and when that day

RICHFORD HOTEL   ROCHESTER, N.Y.

ENJOY
THE FRIENDLY
COMFORTS
OF THE
RICHFORD

MODERN
FIREPROOF
ECONOMICAL

350 ROOMS

ELM & CHESTNUT STS.
HAMILTON 5500

②

comes from then on your going to be with
me every minute. I won't let you
out of my site for one second either.

How about an account of what
I've been doing since I last wrote you.
I wrote you yesterday at about 2.00 pm, then
we went to see a disc jockey, from there I went
to the club to do some musical arrangements,
(which I found very hard to do because I was
thinking of you all the time.) At 6.30 pm I
went out and had something to eat.
Then off to the club for the 9.00 oclock show.
The last show was at 12:30, then Pat and
I went and had something to eat, and
then went right to bed at about 2:00. We

RICHFORD HOTEL   ROCHESTER, N.Y.

ENJOY
THE FRIENDLY
COMFORTS
OF THE
RICHFORD

MODERN
FIREPROOF
ECONOMICAL
550 ROOMS

ELM & CHESTNUT STS.
HAMILTON 5500

(3)

were all up at about 7:30 AM. We had to go
and see one of the morning disc jockeys. Then
after that, guess what, we went and played
golf with another disc jockey in town here.
Got back to the hotel about 2:00 pm. I slept
for about an hour, and now I'm writing
this letter to you.

Honey everybody that I've told
about us, and I've told almost everybody
I speak to, after I've told them all about
you, say that I couldn't have found a
nicer girl, and Pat Ray + Johnnie told
me that they hope some day they can meet
a girl like you. I guess I'm the lucky
one. Please, honey don't ever leave me.

Darling, I'm glad that you believe
in me, and trust me the way you do, because
honey I will never be unfaithful to you in
any way, never hurt you. I promised you
that while I'm away I'll never take out
another girl or have any dates, and I meant it.
I love you very very much, and your letters
and the times when I phone you are the only
things I look forward to.

       Honey, I want you, if you
possibly can, to come to Canton, and I'll
phone you Tuesday morning at about 9 or 9:30
maybe you'll know by then. We'll talk about
the expense of it then also. Don't worry about
the money, we'll arrange something. As long
as you can get the week-end off, the rest of it

RICHFORD HOTEL   ROCHESTER, N.Y.

ENJOY
THE FRIENDLY
COMFORTS
OF THE
RICHFORD

MODERN
FIREPROOF
ECONOMICAL

350 ROOMS

ELM & CHESTNUT STS.
HAMILTON 5500

(5)

we can arrange.

    The pictures you sent to me
were tremendous. Ever since I got them
I look at them 24 hrs a day. Last night
I went to sleep looking at them, and every
night at 1:00 o'clock I'm going to look
at them in a very special way and say
over and over, I love you.

    Well this has been a real
long letter, honey, I hope I didn't make
it too long, but when I write to you I
could write forever.

      Thinking About You Always

All my love —
      Always & Forever
        Rudi

P.S. my love to all the gang.

Canton, Ohio: End of May

I wrote to Rudi every day. Jo and I did get to Canton, Ohio. Our plane arrived early, and the cabbie told us that the auditorium where the Crew-Cuts were appearing for a special teen show was only about ten minutes away from the hotel. Jo suggested she take the bags and check in for us, and that I should go and surprise Rudi. As I arrived in the lobby, I heard the end of "Sh-Boom" and the screams of the teen-agers.

The guys came out through the double door, with all the kids following. They stopped and signed autographs. When Rudi signed, I noticed he tried to make eye contact with the person, which I thought was very nice. I got in line, and said, "May I have your autograph?" Rudi looked up and his smile was wonderful as he realized it was me. Just from the look in his eyes at that moment, I knew that everything he had written me in all those letters (two a day) was true and sincere.

He took my hand, as I waved to the others, said "See you later!" and we ran out together. We were so happy to see each other.

Jo and I had a great time, but Monday afternoon came very quickly. Our weekend was over, we were off, and the Crew-Cuts were headed to Chicago.

I was studying for finals, doing case study papers. Graduation was in September. When we got back from our trip, the girls were all waiting to grill us. What outfits did the Crew-Cuts wear, what outfits did we wear? Was it fun going out to dinner with them? Did people recognize them? Did they think you were a singing duet, or an opening act? The questions they came up with! Rudi called that night, still so thrilled that I'd been able to be there.

My next trip to see Rudi would be when the group appeared in Cleveland, and it was very hard trying to keep my mind on studying and writing papers. I just wanted to work my shift, then sit and write and dream of Rudi. He was so kind and considerate, and I was so in love. It was like a fairy tale, but I was always being brought back to reality by my studies.

The first few weeks, every time I went to my mail box I had an entourage. They couldn't believe anyone could get two letters a day, sometimes three. Other boyfriends, I was afraid, were going to be in trouble, because one letter a week just wouldn't do from now on.

I was envied by every student nurse – but in a nice way. Let me explain; it wasn't just because Rudi was a Crew-Cut, or the romantic way in which we met. It was the guy himself. He sent autographed pictures, records, albums, and thank-you notes for calling D.J.'s. What really got to the girls was at the end of the note, he would write, "Take care of my girl, I love her very much. Thank you, Rudi."

ALLERTON HOTEL

1:00 P.M. June 1 54

My Dearest Plus;

Just arrived in Chicago, and woo what a drive. We left right after the dance, that was about 2:00 A.M. and we just got here.

I'm not going to make this letter too long, honey, because we have to rush and be over at the Mercury office for rehearsal in about an hr, but I promised you I'd write you as soon as I got here, so here I am.

ALLERTON HOTEL

701 NORTH MICHIGAN AVENUE
CHICAGO 11

②

Darling I'd like to say.
that last week-end was the most
enjoyable week-end I've ever spent.
I hope that very soon I can have you
with me all the time, believe me
when I say that I want to marry
you as soon as possible. I love you
so very very much.

Well, darling I have to
rush and get ready now, I'll call you
at about 7:30 after our rehearsal. I just
can't wait till I speak to you
and I'll write you a real long.

(3)

letter after rehearsal also.

    Plus, darling I can't express
in words, how much I really love
you I wish I could, but I can say
your all I've ever wanted, please
trust and believe in me, and darling
please never leave me. I love you
so very very much

        All My Love – Always & forever

        Judi

R.C.A RADIO SPEAKER
IN EACH ROOM

1000 OUTSIDE ROOMS IN THE HEART OF THE NEW
"MAGNIFICENT MILE"

ALLERTON
HOTEL

701 NORTH MICHIGAN AVENUE
CHICAGO 11

June 2-57 1:00 AM

My Dearest Plus;

Well darling I just got back to the hotel. We've been rehearsing since about 8:00 o'clock till about 12:30 AM for our record session. and boy am I tired.

I'm real glad I was able to talk to you to-nite. It made me feel real good. I love to hear your voice. I gives me a real warm feeling inside

Plus, after seeing you this week-end I know for sure that I want to marry you as soon as possible. Your the only girl for me. I love you so very much, and I need you. Your

JOHN P. HARDING
Hotel
MANAGEMENT
KEN WILLIAMS, Man. Dir.

my whole life now. If I ever lost you
I don't know what I'd do. Please, be
mine always. I need your love so badly.

I guess I should give you
an account of to-day activities. All righty.
Well after driving all nite we arrived
en Chicago about 1ᵃᵐ (by the way we an
hour behind you here). We then checked in
at the hotel. got cleaned up, and went
over to the Mercury office, talked to the big boy
over here, rehearsed a bit till about 6⁰⁰ᵖᵐ. Then I
came back to the hotel, called you about 7³⁰ᵖᵐ.
After I finished talking to you, I went and had
something to eat, then we all went over to
the Mercury office again and rehearsed
till about 12³⁰ᴬᴹ. Went and had

R.C.A RADIO SPEAKER
IN EACH ROOM

1000 OUTSIDE ROOMS IN THE HEART OF THE NEW
"MAGNIFICENT MILE"

ALLERTON
HOTEL

701 NORTH MICHIGAN AVENUE
CHICAGO 11

(3)

a bite to eat. Then came back to the hotel.
Got ready for bed, and I'm now
writing you.

Well I guess that's all the news
for now except that our record session
starts at 7 P.M. on Thursday, and our new record
should be out in about a week.

Darling before I close I'd like to
tell you again, that I'm being real true to you
in every respect. I promise you I will not
take out any girls or have any dates at all. All
I want is you. So please believe and trust in
me. I know you do and that's why I will never
hurt you in any way

R.C.A. RADIO SPEAKER
IN EACH ROOM

1000 OUTSIDE ROOMS IN THE HEART OF THE NEW
"MAGNIFICENT MILE"

**ALLERTON
HOTEL**

701 NORTH MICHIGAN AVENUE
CHICAGO 11

(4)

Well Plus darling I'll close
now, Give my love to all the gang and
don't forget I'll be calling you Saturday
night from Youngstown Ohio.

All my Love – Always & Forever

Rudi

P.S. I'll give you my address for Youngstown
again. It is

Blue Crystal Nite Club
Gerrard Ohio

R.C.A. RADIO SPEAKER
IN EACH ROOM

1000 OUTSIDE ROOMS IN THE HEART OF THE NEW
"MAGNIFICENT MILE"

ALLERTON HOTEL

701 NORTH MICHIGAN AVENUE
CHICAGO 11

June 3-54 12 30

My Dearest Pbus;

Well darling another day is
thru, and boy what a hectic day this
was. I'm sure glad its over.

I got up about 9 30 A.M. this morning
or should I say yesterday morning) mailed
your letter, and then wrote the music out
for our recording session till about
12:30, then we all went over to Mercury
records, and between rehearsing, writing
out orchestrations, discussing how the
tune should be done and what

R.C.A. RADIO SPEAKER
IN EACH ROOM

1000 OUTSIDE ROOMS IN THE HEART OF THE NEW
"MAGNIFICENT MILE"

ALLERTON
HOTEL

701 NORTH MICHIGAN AVENUE.
CHICAGO 11

②

tunes we are going to do, we never left
there till 9:00 P.M. We managed to grab a
sandwich in between tunes, but boy it
was a real hassle. Then Pat, Ray & I
went to a movie, while Johnnie stayed
in and wrote a few letters, (he takes care
of all the business correspondence in the group
and he was pretty far behind). We just
got back, and I am now writing you

Our record session is 7:00 P.M.
to-nite, and our new record should be out
next week sometime, that is the disc jockey
will have, but it probably won't
go on sale for another two weeks,

R. C. A RADIO SPEAKER
IN EACH ROOM

1000 OUTSIDE ROOMS IN THE HEART OF THE NEW
"MAGNIFICENT MILE"

ALLERTON HOTEL

701 NORTH MICHIGAN AVENUE
CHICAGO 11

But I promise as soon as it comes out, I'm sending you two records. One for you, and one for the gang as I promised.

Darling I want you to know that I'll love you forever & always. It hurts me so much to be away from you. I hope that we can get married real soon because I want you near me always. I can't do without you. Oh Plus darling I pray night & day that you'll be always mine, and that I'll never lose you. Life wouldn't be worth living if I didn't have you. Please be mine always. I love you so much.

Well, I guess I'll close now. I'll write again this afternoon

R. C. A. RADIO SPEAKER
IN EACH ROOM

1000 OUTSIDE ROOMS IN THE HEART OF THE NEW
"MAGNIFICENT MILE"

**ALLERTON
HOTEL**

701 NORTH MICHIGAN AVENUE
CHICAGO 11

and don't forget, I'll phone you on
Saturday at about 7:30 p.m. All my love
to all the gang, and I was real
glad to hear you did so good in your
finals, you certainly deserve it.

All my love
Always + forever

Rudi

JOHN R. HARDING
Hotel
MANAGEMENT
KEN WILLIAMS, Man. Dir.

HOTEL FORT WAYNE

300 OUTSIDE ROOMS WITH BATH

AIR CONDITIONED ROOMS WITH TELEVISION AVAILABLE

June 9-51 - 10:00 P.M.

My Dearest Plus;

Well, darling I received something
in the mail to-day that's going to get a real special
spot in my scrap book. Guess what it was?
A real terrific card from three wonderful gals
the girl I love, and two the greatest friends a
person could have. Thanks very much darling.
you don't know how much myself +
the other guys really appreciated it. It was terrific
They all say thanks a million. The record can't
help but hit in Pittsburgh now.
Well, as you know Plus, darling
we finish here on Sunday. We leave here
Monday morning and before we go into New
York we're going to stop off a Philadelphia

CASS AVENUE AT TEMPLE ★ DETROIT 1, MICHIGAN
NEXT TO MASONIC TEMPLE
Telephone TEmple 1-8600

HOTEL FORT WAYNE

300 OUTSIDE ROOMS WITH BATH
AIR CONDITIONED ROOMS WITH TELEVISION AVAILABLE

for a few days to get the new record moving, but I let you know exactly what we're going to do when I phone you on Saturday.

It's about 10 am here and I'm just getting ready to go to the club, we only do one show here and we don't have to be at the club 'til about 11:30 pm. We go on about 12:30 am. We were up at 9:00 o'clock this morning to make our tour of the disc jockeys here and we just got though a little while ago. Whew, what a hectic day.

What are your chances of coming to Lorraine Ohio, Do you think you can possibly make it that week-end. I want you to come so badly if it won't interfere with your work at the hospital. I miss you so very

CASS AVENUE AT TEMPLE ★ DETROIT 1, MICHIGAN
NEXT TO MASONIC TEMPLE
Telephone TEmple 1-8600

HOTEL FORT WAYNE

300 OUTSIDE ROOMS WITH BATH
AIR CONDITIONED ROOMS WITH TELEVISION AVAILABLE

much. If you can come, and there financial difficulty
that's no problem. Just let me know, and I'll take
care of it.

      Well darling I'm going to close now.
May God bless you always, and keep you mine
forever. I love you so very much. Your
so lovely and sweet, and beautiful and wonderful,
I could go on forever, and never stop. I'll love
you forever + a day. I'll write again after the
show to-nite

      All my love — Always & Forever
        Rudi

P.S. I can hardly wait till I phone you on
Saturday.

HOTEL FORT WAYNE

300 OUTSIDE ROOMS WITH BATH
AIR CONDITIONED ROOMS WITH TELEVISION AVAILABLE

June 10-57 10ᵖᵐ P.M.

My Dearest Plus,

I've got a bit of time before I leave for
the club, so I thought this was the best time to
write to you.

I'm real glad that you like the new
record. We are hoping it will be as big as
"Crazy Bout Ya," but naturally "Crazy Bout Ya"
I eds a special meaning to both of us. It
brought you to me forever. We will certainly
have some story to tell our children.

What's with Barry Kaye, he should
be playing our record quite a bit. Oh Well
you can never tell what goes on in the
minds of dese jockeys. There very funny people

CASS AVENUE AT TEMPLE ★ DETROIT 1, MICHIGAN
NEXT TO MASONIC TEMPLE

Telephone TEmple 1-8600

HOTEL FORT WAYNE

300 OUTSIDE ROOMS WITH BATH

AIR CONDITIONED ROOMS WITH TELEVISION AVAILABLE

Real glad to hear the other disc jockeys are
playing it quite a bit though.

Darling we'll be in Philadelphia
for a few days at the first of next week, before
we go into New York to do the Barry Kaye Show.
We're going to do some promotion down there. I
don't know where I'm going to stay there, but
I'll phone you as soon as I get there. I don't
think I'll be able to receive any of your letters
there because by the time your letters would
get there I'll be gone. I'll know more about it
when I phone you on Saturday, at home, Then I'll tell
you exactly where to write

Darling you'll never have to
worry about me. I'll always love you

CASS AVENUE AT TEMPLE ★ DETROIT 1, MICHIGAN
NEXT TO MASONIC TEMPLE

Telephone TEmple 1-8600

HOTEL FORT WAYNE

300 OUTSIDE ROOMS WITH BATH
AIR CONDITIONED ROOMS WITH TELEVISION AVAILABLE

(3)

forever & always. I never want to lose you.
My whole life is yours. I just can't wait
till we can get married, and spend the rest of our
lifes together. I love you so very very much.

Darling I'm real tired, this Detroit
is a real work house. After the show last night
I went right to bed + was up at 8:00 A.M., and
honestly after seeing disc jockeys + visiting record
stores + meeting record distributors we didn't
get through till about a half an hr ago, that
was about 9:30 P.M., and the same schedule is on
for to-morrow. Who said this was a soft life.
Like I said I've seen so many disc jockeys
that I count them when I go to sleep
instead of sheep.

CASS AVENUE AT TEMPLE ★ DETROIT 1, MICHIGAN
NEXT TO MASONIC TEMPLE

HOTEL FORT WAYNE

300 OUTSIDE ROOMS WITH BATH
AIR CONDITIONED ROOMS WITH TELEVISION AVAILABLE

④

Well darling I've got to rush now to
leave for the club. I'll write again before
I go to bed to-nite. All my love to the Gang.

All My Love — Always & Forever

Rudi

Chapter Four

SUMMER LOVE

CHAPTER 4: SUMMER LOVE

June, 1954: Cleveland

*M*o and I flew into Cleveland and went directly to the Westlake Hotel on the lake shore, a beautiful resort. It was the first time we'd ever sat around at a pool, just relaxing. We didn't have much time, because I went with Rudi to all the group's rehearsals, visits to D.J.s, and appearances at record stores. He offered to let Mo and me stay at the pool and relax if we wanted to, but I knew that he wanted me with him, and we had so little time together. I could sun almost any time, and the purpose of the trip was to be together. The time went so fast that weekend. We had a ball. Jo and I would be in Lorain in a week and a half for the 4th of July, and Rudi would join us.

My family would all be there and we'd have such a great time. Rudi was so excited to meet everyone. I grinned to myself, thinking that he had no idea what he was in for. Six of my seven uncles would be there to check him out.

The Crew-Cuts worked very hard. Their popularity was growing, but in order to get ahead and keep ahead, it was work, work, work. Rudi didn't care how hard he worked, he said, because when I was there it was fun. And I loved watching him.

The Crew-Cuts had started as a group in Toronto, where they charted their first records. They had all been members of the St. Michael's Choir School in Toronto, which also spawned another famous quartet, The Four Lads. Rudi Maugeri, John Perkins, and two others (Bernard Toorish and Connie Codarini) who later were among The Four Lads first formed group called The Jordonaires (not to be confused with a similarly named pop group, The Jordanaires, that was known for singing backup vocals on Elvis Presley's hits) and also The Otnorots ("Toronto" spelled backwards being "Otnorot"), but they split from the group to finish high school.

When The Four Lads returned to Toronto for a homecoming concert, John Perkins and Rudi ran into each other and decided that they could have a musical future together. They joined with Pat Barrett and Ray Perkins in March 1952. The group was originally called The Four Tones (not to be confused with The Four Tunes, a group on the borderline between pop music and rhythm and blues).

In March 1953, they returned to Toronto and appeared as an opening act for Gisele MacKenzie at the Casino Theater. She was impressed with them and commented favorably to her record label, but could not remember the group's name!

They were playing in a Sudbury, Ontario night club in a sub-zero Canadian winter when they received notice that they had been invited to appear as guests on a Cleveland television program. They drove 600 miles at -40 degree temperatures to appear on the Gene Carroll show, where they remained for three appearances and also while in Cleveland met local disk jockey Bill Randle. On his show, on Cleveland AM radio station WERE, he coined the name that would from that point on belong to the group. The name "Crew-Cuts" refers to their short hair, as opposed to long hair, which at the time implied classical music. It was a decade later that long hair came to be associated with the counter-culture movement. In addition, Randle arranged for them to audition with Mercury Records, who liked them enough to sign the quartet to a contract.

Although their first hit "Crazy 'Bout Ya Baby" was written by Rudi and Pat Barrett themselves, they quickly became specialists at cover recordings of original R&B songs. Their first cover "Sh-Boom" (of which the R&B original was recorded by the Cords) hit number one on the charts in 1954. A number of other hits followed, including "Earth Angel" which rose to the number two spot on the charts and had great success in England and in Australia.

Hotel Forrest

224 WEST 49th STREET • NEW YORK 19, N. Y.

CABLE ADDRESS "FORESTOTEL"
TELEPHONE Circle 6-5252

June 16, 1954 7:15 P.M.

My Dearest Plus:

Well darling we arrived in New York last night at about 1:30 A.M. and this is the first opportunity I had to write. We flew in from Detroit, and boy that flying is real crazy, there's nothing like it. We previously had planned to go to Philadelphia for a few days, but our manager called us and told us to go straight to New York, because we have an early morning T.V. show to do here. So off we went.

You know, darling, there's nothing like New York. You seem like your in a different world entirely. I wish you were here

with me. Darling we could have such
a wonderful time. Its truly a wonderful
city. We'll just have to come here to-gether
Read soon I hope to.

What a hectic day to-day was.
I got up about 9:30 this morning and Pete
I (Johnnie & Ray don't arrive till to-nite) just
visited the Mercury office, then rushed down to
meet the record distributor here, and then off
to C.B.S. T.V. Studios for rehearsal for the T.V.
show to-morrow morning. We got out of there
about 1:00 p.m. I grabbed a bite to eat, and then
went down to meet the publisher who published
"Crazy Bout ya" and the publisher whose
publishing the ballad on our new
record. We got through here about
3:30 p.m. Rushed down to visit our
booking office M.C.A. Stayed

(3)

here for about an hr, and came back to the
hotel and then had dinner. Well that
brings me up to date.

Our new record is going real
great. Everyone has picked it to hit, and
the disc jockeys here in New York really
like it, so we've been told. The records should
be in the stores to-morrow. So if they are
I'll send you the two I promised to-morrow.
All Righty. "Crazy Bout ya" is real strong
here in New York, and this is one place where
everybody is real critical, but we've been lucky
all the people we've visited seem to think the
world of us so I think even in pretty
solid in the "big city."

Well darling we've got the
evening off to-nite, before we hit
the grind to-morrow. We have

to be up at about 7.00 o'clock to-morrow morning for the T.V. show, and from then on we start our tour of the d.j's here. Pat + I are going to a movie or maybe the ball game, to-nite and get to bed real early because we'll have to get up about 6.00 o'clock to-morrow.

I'll close now. Plus darling, I'll be calling you to-morrow around 10 P.m. I can hardly wait till then. Plus darling please pray that everything will go real great so that we can get married in about 10 or 11 months. I miss you so very much. I just can't do with out you. Your my whole life. I

I'll write again after the movie to-nite. All my love to the gang.

All my love
Always + Forever.

Rudi

CENTRALLY LOCATED
Air Conditioned Rooms

P.S. As soon as you get this letter, you can write to the above address. I'll wait for a letter before I leave here.

June 17-54 1:00 A.M.

My Dearest Plus,

I just got back from the movies. Just saw a real terrific picture, Dial M for Murder. I really enjoyed it. Well I have to get up real early this morning about 6:00 A.M. as I mentioned in my last letter we have an early morning T.V. show to do from 7 till 10. Who watches T.V. that early? Who cares we're getting paid for it!

Darling right after the T.V. show I'll be calling you, and I can hardly wait to hear your wonderful voice. I hope that pretty soon, I won't have to be calling you anymore, but that you'll be right here with me all the time. I love you so very very much. I just hope

Hotel Forrest

224 WEST 49th STREET • NEW YORK 19, N. Y.

CABLE ADDRESS "FORESTOTEL"
TELEPHONE CIrcle 6-5252

(2)

pray that everything goes as we planned, and that we'll be together always. I could never love anyone else but you ever. I want you to be mine always.

Well we've got a real hectic week ahead of us. Besides visiting the d. j's and record stores. We have to do a big teen-age show here on Friday night, plus the show with "Barry Kaye" at the new Yorker Hotel on Saturday + a big net Work Radio Show on Sunday, the guy that's running it is "Eddy Gallagher". You might be able to get this in Pittsburgh. I'm not sure though.

How is Sh Boom going in Pittsburgh. Is Barry Kaye still playing the chords. If he is, just cross him off your list. All the big music magazines have picked it to hit. One magazine called "Cash Box" had our pictures in it and picked Sh Boom to hit

CENTRALLY LOCATED

Air Conditioned Rooms

the top ten. It's hope it's right.

Well Plus darling how is everything going with you. Real wonderful I hope, and you better be getting lots of sleep and taking good care of yourself. That's an order. Okay!

How is everything for Cleveland. You'll be able to come, I hope. I just have to see you and hold you in my arms, and tell you I love you. I'm praying real hard so that you'll be able to come.

Well I'll close now darling I'll write again to-morrow.

all my love
always + Forever

Rud

4th of July

July 4th was going to be a big weekend. The Crew-Cuts were appearing at the Showboat in Lorain, Ohio. Most of my mother's family now resided there. Mother and Charlie were coming from Uniontown to meet Rudi. I would have two and a half days off.

I was packing and unpacking, then repacking, because I had to have just the right outfits.

A couple of days before leaving, I was working the 2:30 to 11:00 P.M. shift. Because of an emergency, I didn't get off 'till after midnight. The next day, I was scheduled to work from 7 in the morning to 3:30 in the afternoon, and I had to be up at 5:30 A.M.

My roommate Les was on nights. I was so tired that I slept through my alarm, missed chapel, and I lost my privileges. I could not believe it! I was hoping that maybe they'd missed roll call, but no such luck; the slip was in my mailbox when I got off duty, stating that my privileges for the coming weekend were revoked. I immediately called my nursing advisor, Miss McD, explained the family reunion, begged to have no privileges for the next couple of weeks if they would just reinstate this coming weekend. No? Well, I would go anyway, I would quit if I had to.

Fortunately, I called Rudi first. He was shocked and disappointed, but took the more mature viewpoint. Next call was to my mother, who tried to calm me; sure, it was disappointing but there would be next weekend, and I couldn't jeopardize everything I had worked so hard for.

(She did not know at this time how I got out to meet Rudi. That story would be told after graduation, and I was sure it would not be well received.)

I sulked all weekend, even though I did receive many calls from Rudi. The house mother did do a bed check on my two nights; once she found me in the shower, and I had to stick my head out so she could be sure it was really me. The next night, I was sitting in bed reading and, as she peeked in, I just smiled and gave a little wave. They were all very nice ladies; they were just doing their jobs.

The appearance at the Showboat in Lorain was a big success. My whole family went to see them. One of the cousins was playing in the band. My mom and Charlie came to meet them and introduce themselves, but would not stay, planning to wait until I could be there. Rudi said he recognized my mom immediately, as we looked so much alike. My aunt and uncle had the Crew-Cuts over for dinner, of course, with many of the relatives. The guys really enjoyed home cooking.

I arrived in Lorain very late the following Saturday. My uncle picked me up at the train. I was in time for the last show. This was the end of the second week at the Showboat. The club was standing room only, and very hot.

Early Monday morning, we all drove to Pittsburgh, the Crew-Cuts to promote their record and me for one early afternoon class. After class, I was free until they left. I would sleep a few hours, and then be on duty at 11 P.M. This Monday was a bonus and helped make up for the previous week.

Lorain Paper July 1954

Shaping those Crew-Cuts.

Now, #1 in the Country.

The
Antlers Hotel
WASHINGTON & W. ERIE AVENUE
LORAIN, OHIO

PHONE:
LORAIN 22351

R.O. MOLES
MANAGER

7/5 — 3:00 A.M.

My Dearest Plus;

Just got home from the club dancing and boy am I glad to get back to the hotel. Wow it was so jammed in there to-nite for the first two shows we could hardly breath, but it makes us feel good to have all those people still waiting even though this is our 2nd. week.

To-day I didn't get up till about 1 P.M. this is the first day in a long time that I've slept this late. I got up, had a bite to eat. Then I went over to the club and did some more work on some new numbers. I left the club about 4:00 P.M.) came back to the hotel, and did some cleaning up I went thru my suitcase, got all my write ups & ads etc, and put them in order so I can paste in my scrapbook. I finished that about 6 P.M. I then went and had

DINING ROOM   MODE BEAUTY SHOP   COCKTAIL LOUNGE

The
Antlers Hotel

WASHINGTON & W. ERIE AVENUE
LORAIN, OHIO

PHONE:
LORAIN 22351

R.O.MOLES
MANAGER

②

something to eat, came back to my room, and
decided to get cleaned up & go to the Club. Well by
the time I was all cleaned up & ready to go, it
was about 9ºº P.M. So we all went over to the club.
We did four shows to-nite, and believe me I'm
real tired. I won't have any trouble sleeping
to-nite. Well the last show went on about 1³⁰ P.M.
and I was back at the hotel around 2³⁰ P.M. and
I'm now writing you, that brings me right
up to date.

According to your last letter you
were real disappointed about losing this week-end
darling, well I was real disappointed too. because
I was looking forward to seeing you, but it
looks like our plans were spoiled. I know how this
hurt you darling, and it hurt me just as much.
But as I said in my last letter we'll try and
make up for it on monday. and I'll phone you
on Saturday & Sunday that will take a bit of

DINING ROOM • MODE BEAUTY SHOP • COCKTAIL LOUNGE

the loneliness away for both of us.

The
Antlers Hotel
WASHINGTON & W. ERIE AVENUE
LORAIN, OHIO

PHONE:
LORAIN 22351

R.O. MOLES
MANAGER

(3)

Plus, your really a wonderful girl. You
the kind of a girl that guys dream of finding all their lives.
And I was lucky enough to find you. Ever since I've
met you, you've made my life so happy and
so worth living. Plus, darling, I know that we were
meant for each other and that our love is the
real thing. I love you so very very much.
May God bless our love & happiness for the rest
of our lives. I want you to be mine for
always & forever.

I'll close now darling, I'll phone
you on Saturday. I've received three letters from
you all ready this week, two came on Wednesday
& one on thursday. Wow but that sure make me
feel good. You know I know just how much it means
to me to receive your letters. I look forward to each day
then, and like I said before they should deliver mail on
Sunday. So I can receive a letter then also. I'll
write again and that honey.

All my love - Always & forever Rudi

THE PARK SHERATON HOTEL
NEW YORK 19, N. Y.

7/5

2⁴⁵ Am.

My Dearest Plus;

Well darling I'm just getting ready to go to bed, and I'm really tired. We had a real busy day to-day, and boy was it hot here to-day. It was 99° Wow what a day to be visiting disc jockeys, and we just finished up now.

Honey. I want you to know, that I'll never stop loving you the way I do now. Each time I see you, Each time I leave you, my love for you grows + grows. I'll love you this way till the day I die. And please darling don't worry about me meeting different girls on the road I'll always be true to you forever, and no one will ever take my love away from you. I love you so very very much.

Darling I'm not going to make this letter too long, because I'm real tired and I have to get up at 6⁰⁰ Am. It is now 3⁰⁰ Am. We have to drive to davePort Rhode Island for a one-nighter to-morrow night. then on to Asbury Park for the week.

Oh by the way keep writing to Cleveland, till I get
to Asbury Pk, then when I phone you on Saturday
I'll give you the address, and you can write there
I'll close now darling. I'll write again to-morrow

All My Love
            Always & Forever
                    Rudi

July 20, 1951

My Dearest Plus:

Just received another letter from you this morning, and wow that made me feel real good.

I'm real glad that you had a good time at the picnic, and I can understand when you say that something was missing because I feel exactly the same way. I just can't enjoy myself the way I use to without you darling. I've got to have you around all the time, before I'll be really contented & happy. I love you so very very much.

Well darling since I wrote you last, which was about 24 hrs ago, I've been taking it real easy. After I wrote you yesterday, I went down to the "throwing range" and practiced my golf for awhile, then I came back to the hotel, had supper and went over to the pavilion. The shows went over good and we got finished about 12:30, they ran them a little earlier last nite. The other guys had dates, but I went with "Jos Elgart" and "Bob Farine" Jos's manager, to get something to eat, and you know something darling seeing the other guys have dates & that, doesn't even bother me anymore. All I think about is you from morning till nite, and knowing that you love me the way you do is all I need to keep me real happy. I love you so very very much. Well anyway I got to bed about 3:30 A.M. Got up about 12:00 noon — had breakfast. Went down to the golfing range again, came

3.

back & now I.'m writing you.
Well I guess Whats all
for now, honey, I can hardly wait
till I phone you to-nite, and I'll
write again to-nite also.

All my Love
Always & forever

Rudi

My Dearest Blues:

He honey, we just arrived in Allentown, and I've just got a few minutes to scribble off a few lines before we have to rush to the club.

It took us about 3 hrs to drive here from Asbury Pk. and after the show to nite we have to drive right out to Salem New Hampshire It's about 300 miles from here. Wow they sure keep us hopping.

Darling to-morrow nite I'll be able to write again, so if by chance you happen to miss a little one day you know it's because the one nighters keep you going so fast you can hardly write

What about Chicago have

②

you found out what your going
to do. I really do want to see you.
When I call you we'll talk about
it. All righty

I have to run now darling
With this letter I send

All My Love

Always + Forever

Rudi

THE LAURENTIEN
MONTREAL, CANADA

July 27 7⁰⁰/P.M.

My Dearest Plus;

Hi darling we are now in Montreal we
arrived early this morning about 3 30/A.M. We flew in,
and as soon as I checked in at the hotel here I went
right to bed.

I got up about 11 30/A.M. and then we had
to rush down to see the guy who's working on our crossing
papers, after that we went to visit a few disk jockeys
here and arrived back at the hotel here about 5 30/P.M.
and sat down to write you right away.

The "Como Show" with Ray Anthony
went over real great last night, and we really
enjoyed doing it. Ray Anthony is a real great guy
and I think his band is pretty terrific after working
with them last nite.

A SHERATON HOTEL

THE LAURENTIEN
MONTREAL, CANADA
②

I'll be phoning you to-morrow nite around dinner time, and were leaving here to-morrow nite. Were flying to New York, picking up our car, and driving out right away to Chicago. On our way to Chicago we are stopping off in Cleveland for an hour to do a T.V. show with the Four Aces, who I think are working in Cleveland now. Then we should arrive in Chicago early Friday Morning.

With all this travelling darling I'm pretty tired out. I'm real glad to be in Chicago for two weeks.

Darling I love you, I love you, I love you and do hope I can see you very very soon, because I miss you so very very much. I pray every day that the day will come very very soon when we can be to-gether for always & ever. Darling please never leave me, and be with me always. I love you so very very much. It hurts me so very much also to be away from you.

The Laurentien
MONTREAL, CANADA

I'll close now darling I'll write
again later to-nite so till I phone you to-morrow

All My Love
Always & Forever

Rudi

My Dearest Phee;

Well darling please excuse the paper
I'm writing this letter between shows and I
borrowed the paper off the stage hand. I
received one of your letters that you sent here, and
after being without your letters for awhile I sure
felt good.

Darling I'm very unhappy that you
couldn't come down here, but no matter whether
you come or not, I still make believe your
with me all the time. I do love you very
very much, and believe me darling there's no
mistake, being away from the one you love shows
whether you have that true love or not, and I know
for sure that I have. Sometimes I think its a blessing
to be away for awhile because there's no better way
of making sure of yourself, and I'm positively
sure of myself. I love you so very very

much and I know you feel exactly the same
way, so we have nothing to worry about.

This is a real tremendous date & a real
tremendous theatre. You don't know what a thrill it is to
step out on that stage to a full house (and I'm
not bragging darling, but the theatre been packed
ever since we started). This is like a real big
dream darling I hope it never stops. We have a
real great picture on with us, Dean Martin &
Jerry Lewis new picture being there. Also
theres a Latin American Revue, and an emcee by
the name of Paul Gray. All in All it's a well
rounded show.

I'll be calling you in a very short while
honey — I can hardly wait. You don't know what
three phone calls mean to you.

Well I guess that's all for now honey
I'll write again tomorrow.

All my love
Always & Forever
Dad.

My Dearest Plus;

8/2

Darling it was real won-
derful talking to you yesterday.
You really are cute you know
and when I hear that cute
voice of yours. Wow, I feel like
a million dollars. I love you
so very very much.

There's nothing like
playing a theatre date honey.
Although its pretty hard working
them. Yesterday we did sex shows
and between that and making

personal appearances & visiting disc jockeys, we were real beat.

This morning something like a real great feeling of what good we can do in this business came over me. We visited a girl who's dying of Leukemia, and doesn't know it. When she heard we were in town she pleaded with hospital authorities and her mother that she wanted to see us. They got in touch with us and we gladly went down. You should've have seen the expression on her face when we walked in, and when

We sang "Crazy Bout Ya" +
"Sh Boom" to her, and doing it
made me and I think the rest
of the guys feel real great when
we saw how happy we made her.

I was very very sorry to
hear about Jo. I didn't realize
it was so serious till after I
read your letter, tell her to take
real good care of herself. I pray real
hard for her. She's a real great kid.

Well darling we've been
going together for 3 months. I'm
sorry I didn't remember our anniversary
on the phone. I'm so forgetful
I don't know how you put

up with me.

I guess, I'll close now
darling. I love you so very very
much. So till I write again
to-morrow.

All My Love

Always & Forever

Ruth

8/4 / 1 30 P.m.

My Dearest Plus;

Hi, honey. Do you know
I love you very very much.
Well I do and I intend to for
the rest of my life.

Boy were so busy here
I don't know whether were coming
or going. I'm real wacked out.
This is the tiredest I've ever
been or felt. We're doing five shows
a day here and sometimes six. It's
a real workhouse. Besides all
the promotion we're doing.

Some more news. Over
the weekend the manager here
just told us we broke the record
for attendance this yr. It was
set by Milton Berle. Pat Boone
Also this week in Cash Box
Sh Boom moved to the no I
spot. Its now the no I
tune in the country. Darling
I think our group has so much
to be thankful for. I'm starting
to pray harder, and thank the good
Lord for all he's done for us, we're

been real fortunate.

How is Jo feeling, much better, I hope? Let me know in your next letter. And how did you enjoy your week-end. Real great huh.

Well darling that's all the news for to day. I'll write again to-nite, and phone you to-morrow. I love you, I love you, I love you.

All My Love
Always & Forever
Rudi

(over)
(over)

P.S This letter is a bit short, but I'm rushing it so I can mail it right away, and it can get to you faster. I'm writing it between shows.

Love Always
Your guy

Aug 7

My Dearest Plus,

Well darling it's now about
2°° pm. We finised our first show
and were now getting ready
for our second show.

Honey I'm real sorry
I was so out of sorts on the telephone
but I'm so keyed up, that the least
little thing sets me off, and also
darling I'm goofing because I can't
write you as often as I want, and
believe me this really upset me, but
whatever happens, darling

(2)

my feelings for you will never
change I love you very very
much — I want to marry. this
I know for sure. So please bear
along with me, huh, darling thy'll
come a time when this will all
be behind us.

Some more good news, we've
broken every record at the theatre
here for attendance except one, and
guess who, this'el make Mo, happy
"Martin & Lewis".

We're going to start recording
again next week, and were starting,

to get the material ready now there's some real terrific tunes. I'm starting to arrange them now. After the show here last nite. I went over to the Mercury office, and worked on tunes till about 2 30 AM And when I got home, I just dropped into bed.

I was up about 10 AM. this morning and boy I was real tired. Well what can you do, that's life.

I guess that's all the news for now honey. Always remember. You'll be the only girl I'll ever love. Never forget this.

I want you to be mine always

All my Love
Always + Forever

Rudi

P.S. I'll phone you on the
week-end (save a few quid)

August, 1954: Tell us about the Crew-Cuts

I had a great (but short) trip to Boston, and then a day in New Hampshire.

Rudi and I hadn't seen each other in almost seven weeks. The girls all decided this was too long, so they not only convinced me to go, but also helped me plan a surprise visit. Even though their schedule was so busy, I was happily welcomed and was just part of the group. I was working the night shift, and managed to leave for Boston early Wednesday afternoon, returning on Friday afternoon.

When I arrived in the lobby of the residence, I pushed my suitcase aside, signed in, and walked directly to our mailroom. There were five freshman girls just off duty, checking their mailboxes. We said hello as I opened my box. I pulled out three letters, two from Rudi, and one from Mom.

I was smiling and one of the girls (whom I didn't know) said "Is that from the Crew-Cut?"

"Yes."

"Were you just coming back from seeing him?"

"Yes."

WOW! I started to realize then that even people I didn't know were watching when I went away. It hadn't occurred to me that they'd be so interested. I said good bye, got my suitcase, got on the elevator and proceeded to my room. I immediately put on the album and started singing along as I unpacked. My intention was to sleep for a few hours, then go to late dinner before going on duty.

My door was partially open. I thought I heard a knock, and I looked up to see the five girls from the mailroom. I guess I was singing and playing the music so loud I didn't hear them. I invited them to come in. One girl ran to my desk and picked up the 8x10 autographed picture of my Crew-Cuts (see how possessive I was getting!). She asked if I could get them autographed pictures, and they all wrote their names down for me. Next question, as they all sat down on the beds and listened to music, was could I tell them something about each of them? I answered that I'd be glad to tell them a little about these terrific, talented guys who I'd come to know and care about.

Rudi (baritone) is very kind, considerate, exciting. Let me see, and – oh yes, I don't think I mentioned his very sexy brown eyes. He is the oldest of the group by about seven months, now 23 years old.

Johnnie (tenor) is handsome, with a Kirk Douglas cleft in his chin. I think he's probably the most serious member of the group, and always a gentleman.

Ray (bass), John's brother, is about 15 months younger, very cute, laid back, and is always thoughtful.

Last but not least is the adorable Pat (high tenor), with fabulous blue eyes. He is the youngest by about six months. What a great sense of humor, and so much fun!

The girls loved listening to my descriptions along with the music, and they reluctantly left so I could get some sleep.

When Rudi came a few weeks later, he had the five pictures with him and, of course, they were autographed by all four of the group. The girls were delighted.

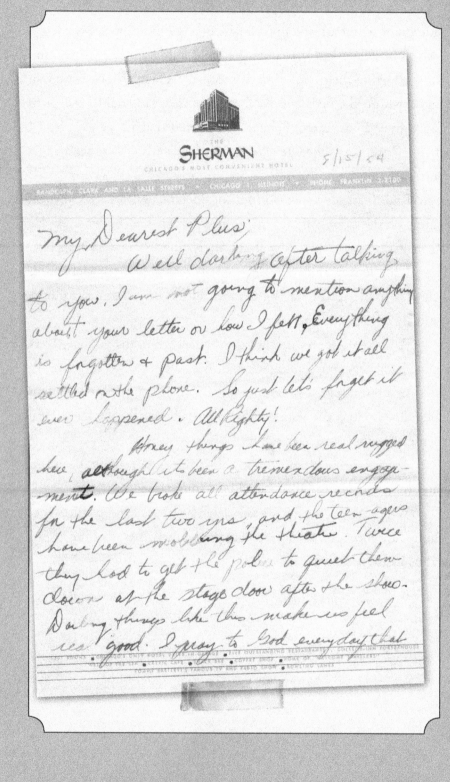

THE
SHERMAN
CHICAGO'S MOST CONVENIENT HOTEL

RANDOLPH, CLARK AND LA SALLE STREETS • CHICAGO 1, ILLINOIS • PHONE FRANKLIN 2-2100

5/15/54

My Dearest Plus;

Well darling after talking to you, I am not going to mention anything about your letter or how I felt. Everything is forgotten & past. I think we got it all settled on the phone. So just let's forget it ever happened. All Righty!

Honey things have been real rugged here, although it's been a tremendous engagement. We broke all attendance records for the last two yrs, and the teen-agers have been mobbing the theater. Twice they had to get the police to quiet them down at the stage door after the show. Darling things like this make us feel real good. I pray to God every day that

6

our success well continue, and that we will always be worthy of it.

How have you been doing darling? How are things going at the hospital? Real great I hope. I also hope your taking good care of yourself, and getting lots of rest, because I don't want you to get sick on me. So don't work too hard. Okay!

Plus darling not hearing from you for almost a week drove me crazy. I love you so very much I can't stand to go without hearing from you for even a day. I love you so very very much

Darling I can also understand that you like myself can really be busy some days so that you can't possibly write. I understand this, and hope that when

THE
SHERMAN
CHICAGO'S MOST CONVENIENT HOTEL

RANDOLPH, CLARK AND LA SALLE STREETS • CHICAGO 1, ILLINOIS • PHONE FRANKLIN 2-2100

I do miss a few days you know it because I frankly
can't write no matter how much I want to.

Well darling I guess I'll close
now. I can hardly wait to call you on Sunday
I'll write again to-night.

All My Love
Always & Forever

Rudi

P.S. My Love to All the Gang.

1301 ROOMS • CHICAGO'S ONLY HOTEL DRIVE-IN GARAGE • FIVE OUTSTANDING RESTAURANTS . . COLLEGE INN PORTERHOUSE
WELL OF THE SEA • CELTIC CAFE • SNACK BAR • COFFEE SHOP • HOME OF "WELCOME TRAVELERS"
TOMMY BARTLETT'S FAMOUS TV AND RADIO SHOW • BOWLING LANES

The CREW – CUTS
Personal Management
FRED STRAUSS

My Guys.

My Dearest Plus;

Well darling, we are now in Hampton beach as you know and we will be here till next Wednesday. Enclosed you will find a list of our future dates a few are being changed but I'll let you know the changes, as soon as I know.

It was real great talking to you yesterday, although you sounded a bit downhearted. Please darling try to be as cheerful as possible. I know it gets pretty rough at times being away from

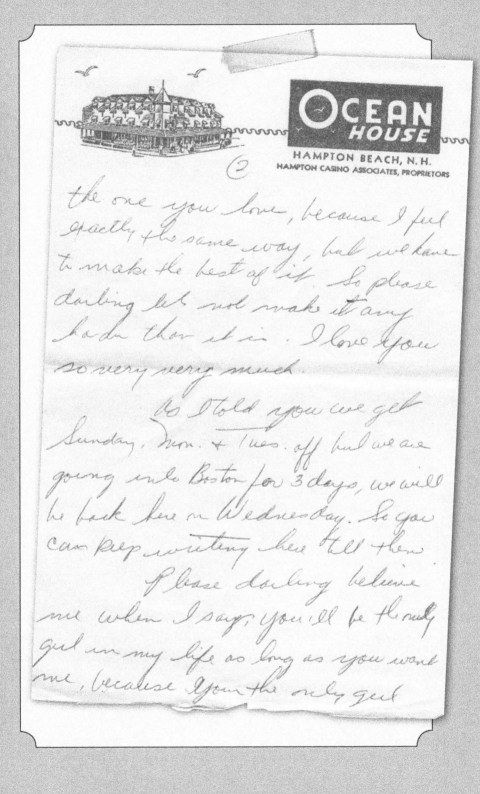

OCEAN HOUSE

HAMPTON BEACH, N.H.
HAMPTON CASINO ASSOCIATES, PROPRIETORS

the one you love, because I feel
exactly the same way, but we have
to make the best of it. So please
darling let not make it any
harder than it is. I love you
so very very much.

As I told you we get
Sunday, Mon. + Tues. off but we are
going into Boston for 3 days, we will
be back here on Wednesday. So you
can keep writing here till then.

Please darling believe
me when I say, you'll be the only
girl in my life as long as you want
me, because your the only girl

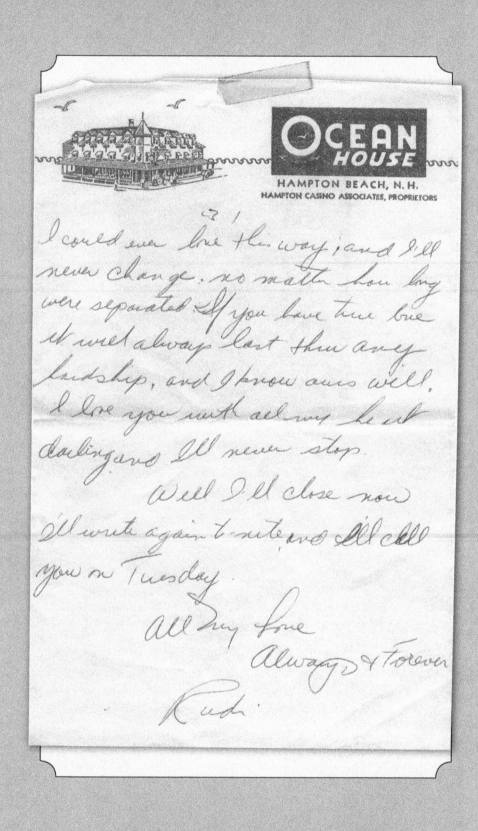

OCEAN HOUSE

HAMPTON BEACH, N. H.
HAMPTON CASINO ASSOCIATES, PROPRIETORS

I could ever love this way, and I'll never change, no matter how long were separated. If you have true love it will always last thru any hardship, and I know ours will. I love you with all my heart darling and I'll never stop.

Well I'll close now I'll write again to-nite, and I'll call you on Tuesday.

All my love
Always & Forever

Rudi

My Dearest Plus;

Hi, honey "look another letter", I've
been a pretty good boy this week huh! this is no
4. So now in your next letter instead of telling
me off, you have to start telling me how good
I've been. All Right;!

Things are going very well here, and
this has been a very enjoyable week. I went to
to bed last night about 3 o'clock. Right after the
last show which is at 1:30 A.M. We do two
shows a nite here. One at 10:30 & the last one
at 1:30. This is a real pleasure after 5 & 6 shows
a day at the Chicago theato. I got up about
11:30 had breakfast, went out shopping again
for about an hr. this time I bought a few sport
shirts, and a bit of baggage, after I came

back we rehearsed for about 2 hrs, and I am
now writing you. We'll finish up here on Friday
nite, then we do 3 one-nighters. Goin to New
York on Tuesday + Wednesday, this time to do the
Eddie Fisher show on T.V. and guess what, we're
taking your advice, we think Oop-Shoop needs
a bit of promotion in Pitts, so we're flying in
sometime on Thursday from New York, and we'll
be there for the day. I don't know exactly what
time we'll arrive or what time we'll be leaving
because we open up in St. Louis on Friday
but I'll know on Saturday, and I'll tell you
then when I phone. I hope it will be possible
to see you for the day. You working nights so
everything should be okay we can spend the

day together. I can hardly wait to see you.
See I talked the boys into it. I love you so
very very much.

Well darling before I close, I'd like
to say I'm thinking of you every minute of
the day. Your my whole life, All my love
is yours. So till I write again tomorrow.

All my love
Always & Forever

Rudi.

One-Day Visit

Rudi and I had talked about their latest release, "Oop-Shoop." I didn't think it was moving fast enough in Pittsburgh. The group decided to take my advice and spend a day in Pittsburgh promoting it.

I guess it was a two-fold suggestion. I really did think the promotion effort was needed. Also, Rudi and I could spend most of the day together.

I was working nights on the men's surgical floor. I arrived on duty at 10:50. The floor was terribly busy and about to get busier. The nurse told me that the orderly would not be coming in, and that I had two critical patients coming up from the emergency room and five pre-ops to have ready by 6:45 A.M. I'd be working the floor alone.

It was a very hectic night, but I was in such a happy mood I didn't mind. In less than twelve hours I would be seeing my guy. My adrenaline kicked in and, with all I had to do, the night passed quickly, even though I did have to stay an extra hour to finish charts.

I skipped breakfast, rushed to the Residence for a shower and a touch of make-up, and in forty minutes I was in a cab on my way to one of the radio stations downtown.

As the cab pulled up in front of the station and I was paying the cabbie, my door flew open and there he was, offering a hand to help me out. Then I was in his arms.

The four of them and I ran from station to station. Rudi and I had an hour and a half for lunch alone together, but unfortunately we spent the time having our first argument. It was over a male friend of mine. Our relationship was strictly platonic, but apparently it had been bothering Rudi.

The group dropped me back at the Residence after we'd had a quick dinner together. They flew off to St. Louis. I was exhausted, and so surprised that Rudi had been jealous for weeks of this friend of mine. I'd never expected this.

We settled everything. The excitement of graduation in the next two weeks was almost overwhelming, and a trip to Milwaukee with five days off compounded my joy.

My Dearest Plus;

Hi honey things are going real great ever since we started the ~~the~~ the people here have taken a real great liking to us. What pleases us though is that they not only like our records but they like our floor show, and we've received some real tremendous compliments. Things like this make us feel real good.

Well this morning I got up about 10 o'clock, had breakfast, and went out to do some shopping with Pat. I bought a new pair of shoes, a suit, a few sport shirts, I also am having another suit made for me in Chicago. So the next time you see me, I should be dressed pretty sharp.

We also bought a couple of new suits for the group, we have now blacksplash suits & grey tuxedos to add to our wardrobe. So we'll all be pretty sharped up when you see us.

After we finished shopping, we come back to the hotel, and rehearsed from 1.00 to 4.00 pm. I then had something to eat, and came upstairs, and I am know writing you. So that brings me right up to date.

Darling I miss you ever so very very much, and I can hardly wait till I see you in October. I love you more & more each day. Your everything to me, and I don't ever want to lose you. I love you so very very much.

Well I guess I'll close now darling I'll write again to-morrow, and I'll be phoning you to-morrow also. So till then

All My Love
Always + Forever.
Ruch.

P.S. Boo! Love you like Crazy.

The JEFFERSON

TWELFTH BOULEVARD AT LOCUST · SAINT LOUIS, MISSOURI

My Dearest Plus;

Well darling it was real wonderful seeing you on thursday. I feel very hurt & sorry that we had to waste a lot of those precious moments arguing, but that was a problem that kept bothering me & bothering me. I just had to let you know about it.

I hope that you got caught up on your sleep on Friday. You seemed real beat when I left you. I felt real sorry for you.

Opening night here was pretty terrific, we had over 1800 people in the ballroom. It was really packed, and everything went real great. My cold was pretty bad yesterday, but I got a lot of sleep & rest last night & it was a lot better to-day.

Well darling to-morrow we have

AIR CONDITIONED · 500 ROOMS

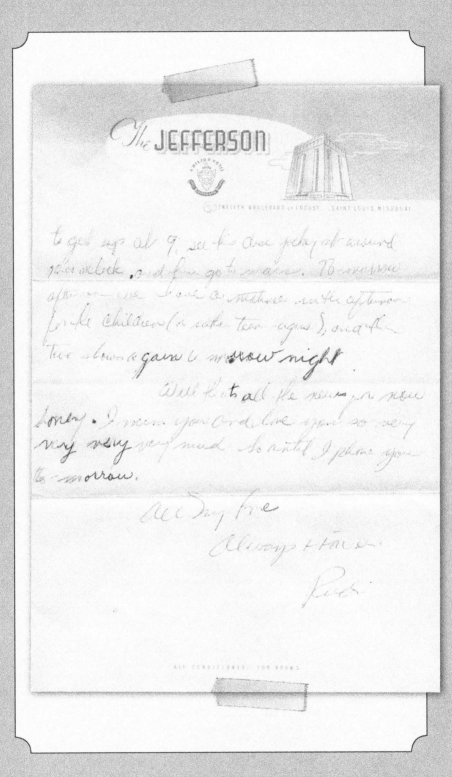

to get up at 9, see the dress rehearsal at around
ten o'clock, and then go to mass. Tomorrow
after — we have one a matinee in the afternoon
for the children (or rather teen agers), and then
two shows again tomorrow night.

Well that's all the news for now
honey. I miss you and love you so very
very very very much. So until I phone you
tomorrow.

All My Love
Always + Forever

Rich

Hotel Muehlebach

KANSAS CITY 5, MISSOURI

My Dearest Plus:

Well darling its Wednesday. Sept.
22, and we have another 10 days here in Kansas
City. It's a real nice city and everybody seems
so friendly & nice.

Darling I'm very sorry I missed
calling you on Sunday, but we had to go
and do a show for the kids at the University
here, and I couldn't get to a phone till about
11:00 pm our time which is 1:00 AM, and then I
knew that was too late. I've called you
several times since, and I just can't seem to
get you your either on duty or have been out
I'm going to try again in a few hrs.

Well darling just two more days
till your graduation, and I'm sending your gift
out to-day. You should get it right on your

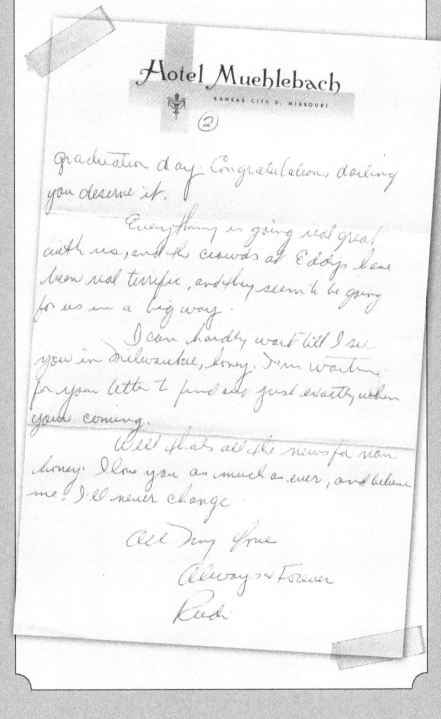

Hotel Muehlebach
KANSAS CITY 5, MISSOURI

②

graduation day. Congratulations darling
you deserve it.

Everything is going real great
with us, and the crowds at Eddys have
been real terrific, and they seem to be going
for us in a big way.

I can hardly wait till I see
you in Milwaukee, honey. I'm waiting
for your letter to find out just exactly when
your coming.

Well that's all the news for now
honey. I love you as much as ever, and believe
me, I'll never change.

All My Love
Always & Forever

Rudi

The CREW-CUTS

1008 HIPPODROME BLDG.
CLEVELAND 14, OHIO
CHerry 1-3713

My Dearest Plus:

Well darling I just finished having supper, and I got about an hr. before I have to get ready for the show to-nite. How is everything going in Pittsburgh, real great I hope, and wow your graduation is to-morrow. Congratulations darling, and all my wishes are for your happiness, now and forever.

I was up at 9.00 o'clock this morning and its been a pretty hectic day. I did some arrangements for our rehearsals then went out to get a haircut, did a bit of shopping, and get back to the hotel about 12.00 noon, the other guys were just getting up, then they went down & had breakfast, when they came back

JOHNNIE PERKINS · RUDI MAUGERI · PAT BARRETT · RAY PERKINS

We went over to the club and rehearsed for a couple of hrs, then Pat & I walked around downtown for a hr. or so, then we had dinner, and came back to the hotel, and that brings me right up to the present. All Righty.

 things are going real great, the club is sold out every nite for the rest of our engagement here, so that makes us feel real good. We're holding to extra matinees on Saturday, so that we can accommodate all the people. I only hope that our popularity will always remain like this. It makes you kind of scared in a way.

 Well darling I hope that you have a real wonderful day to-morrow, I'll try and be with you every minute of the day so that I can sort of join in with you and celebrate. All Righty. And I'll call you to-morrow as I promised. I can hardly wait. I hope you get what I sent you to-morrow. Tried to get it out so that you'd get it right on the day of your graduation. I really hope you do.

I guess I'll close now, honey. With this letter I send All my love to you. I love you so very very much.

All my Love

Always & Forever

Rudi

Chapter Five

A FINE ROMANCE

CHAPTER 5: A FINE ROMANCE

Graduation Day: September 24th, 1954

*I*t was here, and we made it! The whole class (75 of us now) was euphoric. We were dancing and singing in the halls. I missed our Graduation Prom the weekend before, but that was okay. I worked for a friend who decided to go at the last minute.

Flowers arrived that morning from Rudi. He was in Kansas City, Missouri. Later that afternoon, I received a package. I thought, I am not going to open this until he calls before I leave for the ceremony. With all the excitement, that was very hard to do.

My mother and godmother, Marie, were my guests. My godfather Fay, Marie's husband, who I adored, was dying with lung cancer, but he did call me. All of my mother's family was now living in Ohio. I heard from them, but they couldn't be there. It was all right; I knew they were happy for me.

One other obstacle to take care of before the march down the aisle. My roommate, Les, had married Russ six months earlier in a secret wedding. She was now five months pregnant. And, according to the rules, marriage meant immediate expulsion, no questions asked.

We all had to wear our very fitted uniforms to the ceremony. Mo, Jo, and I tried to take out the seams for her, to accommodate her new shape. We were very good nurses but lousy seamstresses, but she made it.

When Rudi called just as we'd planned, fifteen minutes before we were leaving, I told him I was opening the gift with him. He was so moved.

It was a lovely monogrammed cigarette case/ lighter with a beautiful inscription inside.

I asked him to sing the ballad, "Glory of Love," one of my favorites. He sang it over the phone and promised that he would sing it for me that night in the show.

The ceremony was held in the very beautiful First Presbyterian Church in downtown Pittsburgh. It looked so ethereal as we walked down the candlelit aisle.

Dinner with Mom and Marie and many friends and closed this beautiful day, along with the last phone call of the day from my guy.

Congratulations

I liked it when
I saw it ...
I hope you like
it, too,
Because, you see,
I got it
Especially for
you.

all my love
Always + Forever

Rudi

Rudi's Graduation Card.

October, 1954: 1st Trip to Milwaukee

Oh, my excitement at the prospect of this trip! I had been packing for a week. The guys were appearing at this beautiful club in Milwaukee called Fazio's. I really wanted to look my best; after all, I was now a graduate nurse, earning my own money, and leaving from my own apartment, which I shared with Mo and Jo. I was going to be there six days and five nights, my first long trip. We were staying at the Schroeder Hotel, downtown.

A friend and her boyfriend drove me to the airport, and we talked about flying. It was 1954 and she, like many people, had never been in an airplane, although her boyfriend had. Feeling like a real woman of the world, I raved about what a great way it was to travel.

It was a beautiful, sunny fall afternoon. I was to arrive at the club before the first show. An hour or so into the flight, the seat belt sign came on, and the captain told us we were heading into some rough weather. The plane was starting to shake and bounce up and down. All beverages had been picked up. I put out my cigarette, starting to feel anxious.

Outside the window, the lightning was fierce. I was now starting to feel a little more than nervous. To add to my nerves, my seatmate was driving me crazy. When I get uncomfortable, I become quiet. The guy couldn't stop talking, telling me how bad he thought things were. The captain said we would be changing planes. I didn't care where we landed, as long as I could get off of this plane.

The airport was a madhouse, and I had to stand in a long line to get my ticket changed.

After waiting in line for a phone, I kept dialing the club number until, finally, someone answered. I asked for Rudi of the Crew-Cuts, explaining that it was very important I speak to him. Of course, they said he wasn't there. They thought I was a fan. I told them that I was his girlfriend and that, if they didn't give him the message, they would no doubt lose their jobs. I asked them to let him know that my flight had been delayed because of the lightning storm, but that I should be there by 9:00 that night.

The message they gave Rudi was that my plane was hit by lightning, and I didn't know when I was going to get there. When I finally landed, I grabbed a taxi and told the cabbie to please get there as soon as possible. When we pulled up in front of the club, Rudi had someone waiting for me with money for the cab, and someone else taking my suitcase.

I rushed in, and he and the other guys were waiting for me. What a greeting! Ray told me they didn't know what they were going to do. Rudi didn't want to go on until he saw me. They gave a signal to the M.C. that they were ready. I think they were afraid they were going to have to take me on stage with them.

Of course, the show was great, and Rudi couldn't stop looking to the back of the room where I was standing. It was as if he thought I was going to disappear if he looked away.

In the mornings we'd all meet for breakfast in the hotel dining room, and talk over the day's schedule, then get into the red Ford station wagon, Johnnie or Ray driving, and me in the back with Rudi and Pat. They would sing as we went from D.J. to D.J. and to record stores.

Some of my favorite tunes were the repertoire of collegiate songs, which I loved. I knew every word, and I was encouraged to sing along with the four of them, but I was too shy. I only sang with Rudi.

We would try to do some sightseeing in the city while I was there.

Pattie Page came to the club one night to see their show. They talked her into singing her hit "How Much is That Doggie in the Window?" She was great.

As usual, I was too soon on the plane back to Pittsburgh and they were finishing their date there.

Hotel SCHROEDER
MILWAUKEE, WISCONSIN

WALTER SCHROEDER, PRESIDENT

My Dearest Plus,

Well darling I just finished talking with you, and you don't know how much I hated to hang up. Ever since you left, I feel real lost. Darling please believe me when I say I love you so very very much, and I do want to marry you as soon as possible. My love for you has grown so much in the last week that I couldn't bear to ever lose you, or see you with anybody else. that's why I want t get you the engagement ring as soon as I get to Pittsburgh. I want you to be

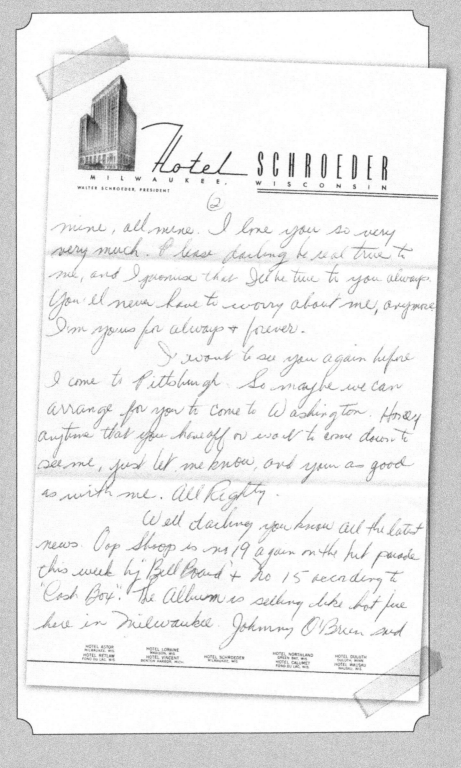

Hotel SCHROEDER
MILWAUKEE, WISCONSIN
WALTER SCHROEDER, PRESIDENT

②

mine, all mine. I love you so very
very much. Please darling be real true to
me, and I promise that I'll be true to you always.
You'll never have to worry about me, anymore.
I'm yours for always & forever.

      I want to see you again before
I come to Pittsburgh. So maybe we can
arrange for you to come to Washington. Honey
anytime that you have off or would to come down to
see me, just let me know, and your as good
as with me. All Righty.

      Well darling you know all the latest
news. Oop Shoop is no 19 again on the hit parade
this week by "Bill Board" & No 15 according to
"Cash Box". The Album is selling like hot fire
here in Milwaukee. Johnny O'Brien said

HOTEL ASTOR
MILWAUKEE, WIS.
HOTEL RETLAW
FOND DU LAC, WIS.

HOTEL LORAINE
MADISON, WIS.
HOTEL VINCENT
BENTON HARBOR, MICH.

HOTEL SCHROEDER
MILWAUKEE, WIS.

HOTEL NORTHLAND
GREEN BAY, WIS.
HOTEL CALUMET
FOND DU LAC, WIS.

HOTEL DULUTH
DULUTH, MINN.
HOTEL WAUSAU
WAUSAU, WIS.

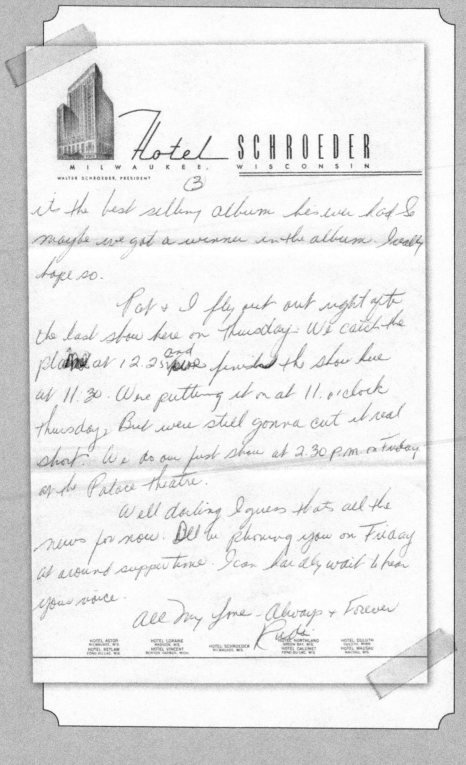

③

it the best selling album he's ever had & maybe we got a winner in the album. I really hope so.

Pat & I fly out out right after the last show here on Thursday. We catch the plane at 12.25 and we finish the show here at 11.30. We're putting it on at 11. o'clock Thursday. But we're still gonna cut it real short. We do our first show at 2.30 p.m on Friday at the Palace theatre.

Well darling I guess that's all the news for now. I'll be phoning you on Friday at around suppertime. I can hardly wait to hear your voice.

All My Love - Always + Forever

Rudi

HOTEL ASTOR
MILWAUKEE, WIS.
HOTEL RETLAW
FOND DU LAC, WIS.

HOTEL LORAINE
MADISON, WIS.
HOTEL VINCENT
BENTON HARBOR, MICH.

HOTEL SCHROEDER
MILWAUKEE, WIS.

HOTEL NORTHLAND
GREEN BAY, WIS.
HOTEL CALUMET
FOND DU LAC, WIS.

HOTEL DULUTH
DULUTH, MINN.
HOTEL WAUSAU
WAUSAU, WIS.

The Bellevue-Stratford

Philadelphia 2, Pa.

CABLE ADDRESS
BELLSTRAT

BENNETT E. TOUSLEY
VICE PRESIDENT AND GENERAL MANAGER

My Dearest Plus,

Well darling I just got home from
the show, and I'm a little tired, We had a real
good nite at the club to-nite, and it seems like
it's going to turn out to be a good week for us, although I was a bit doubtful last nite.

Darling I've come to love you so
much in these last two weeks, that it hurts
me very much when you tell me that your with
Mo & Jo, and your down watching the other group
rehearse, and Mo & Jo asked the boys up to the
apartment & so on. I trust you, darling, don't get me
wrong, I know you would never hurt me, but I feel
that since Mo & Jo are great friends of yours, and

FOR A FRESH START — STOP AT A HOTEL

The Bellevue-Stratford
Philadelphia 2, Pa.

CABLE ADDRESS
BELLSTRAT

⑤

BENNETT E. TOUSLEY
VICE PRESIDENT AND GENERAL MANAGER

your living with them, you sort of go along
with them, and I think at times you shouldn't, and it
unnecessary. I have the same problem with Johnnie
Ray & Pat, but because I'm going steady, if there is
a mixed crowd I don't go along because I'm
going steady. I think you should feel the same
way. If you think I'm asking too much of
you let me know, but that's the way I feel. I
want you to be all mine, darling, and I don't want
anything or anybody to hinder our love for each other.

The Bellevue-Stratford

Philadelphia 2, Pa.

CABLE ADDRESS
BELLSTRAT

BENNETT E. TOUSLEY
VICE PRESIDENT AND GENERAL MANAGER

which I possibly couldn't help. Darling, please believe me when I say you'll get the ring as soon as I get to Pittsburgh. I want to become engaged just as much as you do so please trust my word darling.

Enough lecturing. I'm sorry I had to bring all this up, honey, but I think it's better to tell you how I feel, rather than keep it inside. I know you'll understand. I love you so very very much.

Darling I was disappointed that you couldn't come to Philadelphia this week, but your coming to Washington for sure. I've just got to see you so badly. I miss you so very very much. I can hardly wait till you call on Thursday.

Well I guess thats all the

The Bellevue-Stratford

Philadelphia 2, Pa.

CABLE ADDRESS
BELLSTRAT

BENNETT E. TOUSLEY
VICE PRESIDENT AND GENERAL MANAGER

(4)

news for now. I'll write again to-morrow
this is Your Guy

for Always & Forever

All my Love for Always & Forever

Rudi

P.S My Regards to all the gang.

Love You like mad.

The Bellevue-Stratford

Philadelphia 2, Pa.

CABLE ADDRESS
BELLSTRAT

BENNETT E. TOUSLEY
VICE PRESIDENT AND GENERAL MANAGER

My Dearest Plus:

Well darling its Thursday (actually Friday now) because we just finished our last show, and we've had a pretty successful engagement. I don't know though there's something about Philadelphia that leaves me cold, I'll be glad to leave here.

this morning I was up at 9 o'clock and we worked all morning till about 2.00 p.m. with David Carrol (he flew in last night) to get ready for our recording session on Sunday in Chicago. It's about 2.30 A.M. now, and I have to get up about 9.00 again to do some more work. Oh well that's life.

Oh By the way, darling, in your last letter you mentioned that you were Choreographer & publicity agent for this new group. I just had to mention that your strictly a one group girl, remember, huh! and remember there's a

FOR A FRESH START — STOP AT A HOTEL

The Bellevue-Stratford

Philadelphia 2, Pa.

CABLE ADDRESS
BELLSTRAT

BENNETT E. TOUSLEY
VICE PRESIDENT AND GENERAL MANAGER

a guy in this group by the name of Rudi, who loves you, and he wants you to have only one favourite group, and I think the other guys in the group feel the same way. So how about it huh! We've written a poem.

Pat, Rudi, Johnnie & Ray
Would Always like to hear Phis say
"+ there's only one group that I will boast
that's the Crew-Cuts, I dig them the most."

Let me know how you like it. Pretty bad huh!

Well darling, I guess that's all the news for now. Boy this hotel is the worst. It's suppose to be pretty ritzy, but guess what happened, just before you called to nite, a whole slab of plasta feel down from the ceiling in the washroom. So we called down for the maid, that's who was talking to me when you

The Bellevue-Stratford

Philadelphia 2, Pa.

CABLE ADDRESS
BELLSTRAT

(3)

BENNETT E. TOUSLEY
VICE PRESIDENT AND GENERAL MANAGER

called, you didn't seem to believe me when I told you, but that's the exact truth.

Darling I could never cheat or hurt you in anyway, because I love you so much, that's why I'm demanding so much from you. I'm being real true to you, and I want you to be the same way. I know you are, that's why I love you so much. You know its a pretty hard thing to go steady when you travel, unless you have the right girl, and I have, then it's the most wonderful thing in the world. I love you so very very much.

I guess I'll close now darling. I'll be waiting for your call on Saturday. Don't forget to phone the club later if you can't get me at the hotel when you call, but I'll try & make sure I'm here

All my love— Always & Forever — Your guy - Rudi

October 1954: Washington, D.C.

As the plane was landing, I took the hotel address out of my purse to put in my pocket. Rudi would be waiting for me at the hotel between D.J. visits. I walked from the plane to the terminal. The fabulous summer was over, but fall seemed to be just as great. I was such a lucky girl to be here. We had fallen in love in an instant, "love at first sight."

As I was nearing the terminal, looking through the big window I thought I saw someone waving. Suddenly I realized it was Rudi, and I ran the rest of the way. It seemed I couldn't reach him soon enough. He'd planned to take me sightseeing, since we had three hours before we had to go to the club.

This was my first visit to this historic city. We viewed the White House, the Washington Monument, the Pentagon, and the Smithsonian Museum. I couldn't believe I was there.

Needless to say, three days passed quickly. One of the D.J.s wanted to know who I was, and before I could give my name, Rudi proudly introduced me as his girlfriend and future fiancé. I was speechless, because he always said this to me, but this was the first time he'd said it in public.

Chapter Six

THE ENGAGEMENT

CHAPTER 6: THE ENGAGEMENT

November, 1954: The Ring

*N*ovember started out sadly with the death of my godfather, Fay, at 47. He'd been a flashy, well-known traffic policeman on a busy downtown corner in Pittsburg, and his funeral was a very large military and police affair, so beautifully executed that you felt like you were in a movie. It was the first time I was a part of so much pomp and circumstance, and he certainly deserved the honor. Rudi arrived in Pittsburgh two days after it, and I went to the airport to meet him.

This was our big day in November; the ring. There was a jewelry store called Unger's in downtown Pittsburgh. I used to stare in the window, admiring all the beautiful things. We went in, and I showed him what I had seen in the window. "Are you sure that one is what you want? It's very pretty, but don't you want a bigger ring?"

"No," I said.

It was a carat and a half emerald-cut diamond with a baguette on each side, set in platinum. I thought it was beautiful. He put it on my finger and said, "This is forever. I love you."

We went directly to the apartment to show the roommates. We called my mom, went out to dinner at our favorite restaurant, then met the girls and celebrated. I couldn't take my eyes off the ring or the person who had put it on my finger. We went home the next day to show Mom and Charlie my beautiful ring. Rudi was here for a week. We were ecstatic!

This was Rudi's first trip to Uniontown, and I loved showing him all of my favorite places. St. Mary's Church for the wedding, and the

White Swan Hotel for the reception. My two grammar schools, Ella Peach and St, John's Catholic School. North Union High School, where my four years were great, so many fabulous classmates and friends.

My grandmother's house was out in the country, in Youngstown. The coke ovens were a half mile from her house. They blazed at nighttime, spewing yellow and orange flames up to the sky, where it appeared to meet the stars that sparkled like diamonds. Shady Grove Amusement Park was one mile from her house, where I'd had my first job at 14 at the ice cream stand, and also worked at the roller skating rink selling tickets, learning how to dance on skates.

The Country Club, the stadium where I won the Miss Uniontown Contest, the Summit Hotel. So much to see, so little time. One of my very favorite places was our famous, historic Summit Inn Resort, with its breathtaking views, six miles east of Uniontown. It is a grand "porch" hotel with such charming ambiance, and sits on a mountaintop. It has served such guests as Henry Ford, Thomas Edison, Harvey Firestone, and many others. I had been to several events there, and also had many publicity photos taken after winning the contest. Now I was hoping to get some wedding pictures taken there, too. I showed it to Rudi and he fell in love with it, too. We planned to spend our wedding night there.

I proudly showed off all of these places as if I was personally responsible for them being there.

My Dearest Plen,

Please excuse the pencil. I just now ran out of ink. Well darling we left Chicago at 1:00 pm along with Ralph Martine & Lola Dee. We all are travelling in a big bus. And believe me with all the guys in the orchestra & ourselves, its quite a trip. Anyway, we drove all day & arrived in Green Bay Wisconsin about 8 a pm, did a show & crowd was terrific, left there about 1:30 A.M. drove all night and we just arrived in Madison here at 5 a.m. We play a theatre here tomorrow and we start work at 2:30 pm. We do four shows. Thursday we'll be in Davenport
Friday ... " .. " Edelstein
Saturday ... " .. " Lafayette
Sunday ... " .. " Milwaukee
MONDAY ... " .. " South Bend Indiana

(these are all in Wisconsin I think)

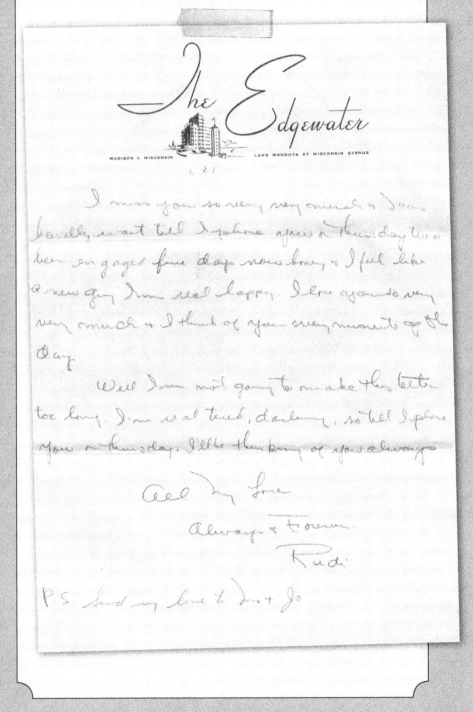

The Edgewater

MADISON 3, WISCONSIN   LAKE MENDOTA AT WISCONSIN AVENUE

I miss you so very, very much & I can hardly wait till I phone you on Thursday. I've been engaged four days now honey & I feel like a new guy. I'm real happy. I love you so very very much & I think of you every moment of the day.

Well I'm not going to make this letter too long. I'm real tired, darling, so till I phone you on Thursday, I'll be thinking of you always.

All My Love

Always & forever,

Rudi

P.S. Send my love to Mom & Jo

TEL. WH 4-4100

Nov 20 - 54

THE SHERATON HOTEL
CHICAGO 11. ILL.

My Dearest Plus

Well darling we are now in Chicago.
We have to do a show in Milwaukee to-nite, then
we're driving back to Chicago, and to-morrow nite
we are in South Bend Indiana at Notre Dame.
from there we go to New York.

Last nite was a real terrific nite
we sang to 11,000 people at Purdue University, and
it was sure a great feeling. All in all the tour with
Ralph Marterie this last week has been pretty
terrific, and everybody seems to be talking
about it we've had real sensational
crowds.

It's now about 5.00 o'clock here in
Chicago, and I tried to call you a little while
ago, but there was no answer I'm going to
try again in half an hr. I hope your
back by then because we're going to have to

TEL. WH 4-4100

THE SHERATON HOTEL
CHICAGO 11, ILL.

leave for Milwaukee pretty soon, and I wanted to call you before we left, because I don't know if I'll be able to call you when I arrive there, everything will probably be so rushed.

Darling ever since we've been engaged, you're more apart of me & everything I do that you can realize. Everything I do, I wish you were here to do it with me. We were truly meant for each other, and believe me darling I can hardly wait till we get married, and I know I've said this before, but now I really mean it, it is going to be as soon as possible because I love you so much, and want you to be with me all the time, that I know I won't be able to wait to long. I love you so very very much.

Well I'll close now darling, I'll try and write again to-morrow, if not Tuesday for sure. All my love — Always & Forever — Your guy
Bill

THE PARK SHERATON HOTEL
NEW YORK 19, N. Y.

My Dearest Plus;

Well darling, happy thanksgiving. You know I've got a lot to be thankful for this year. I'm engaged to the most wonderful girl in the world, and our group has become the top group in the country, what else could a guy ask for. Yep all my prayers were certainly answered. I love you so very very much.

Everything went great on opening nite here, and this New York is really a fabulous city. I think we'll enjoy our stay here. I'm real glad that all the kids like "Dance he Snowman" maybe it'll be a big Christmas hit for us. Let's hope huh.

How are things going in Pittsburgh real great I hope, and I hope that your getting a lot of rest, and eating real good darling, because you work real hard, and you certainly need to keep your stamina up.

Thank all the kids (Dec + Jo) for their thanks on our new record, we all really appreciate it. Things like that make us feel real good.

Well darling that all the news for now. I'll write again to-morrow, and don't forget I'll phone you on Saturday.

All My Love

Always + Forever

Rudi

P.S. I'll send the records out as soon as possible all Righty?

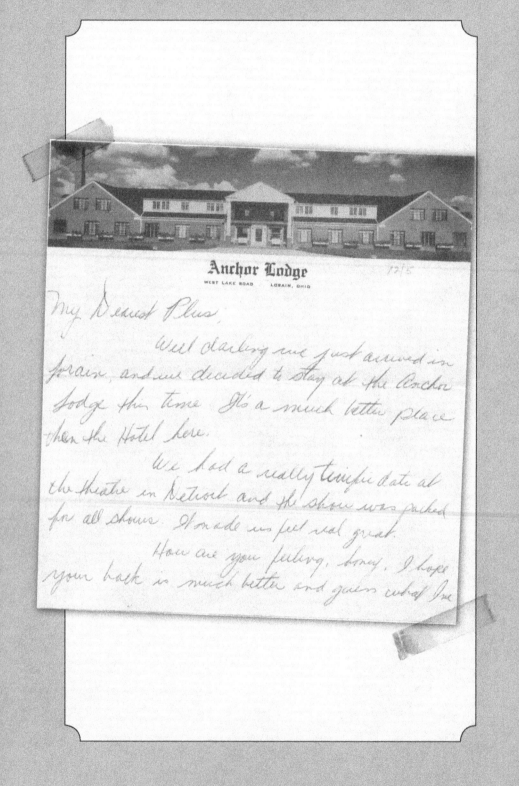

Anchor Lodge

WEST LAKE ROAD · LORAIN, OHIO

12/5

My Dearest Plus;

Well darling we just arrived in Lorain, and we decided to stay at the Anchor Lodge this time. It's a much better place then the Hotel here.

We had a really terrific date at the theatre in Detroit and the show was packed for all shows. It made us feel real great.

How are you feeling, honey. I hope your back is much better and guess what I've

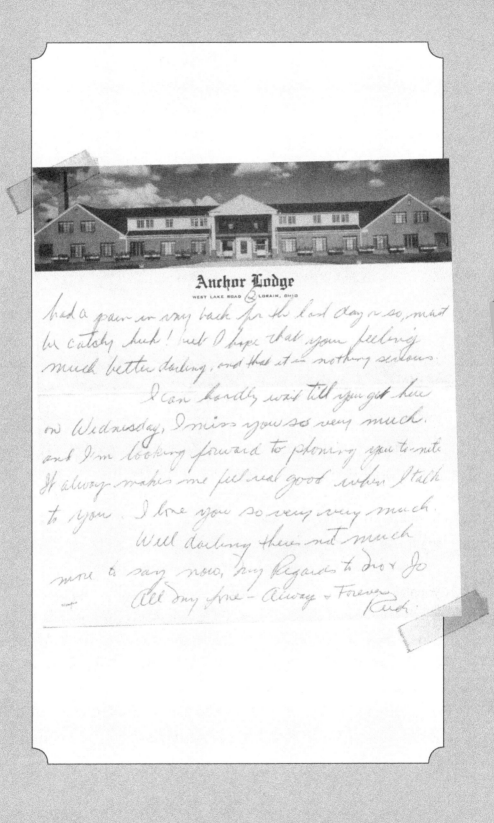

Anchor Lodge

WEST LAKE ROAD 2 LORAIN, OHIO

had a pain in my back for the last day or so, must
be catchy huh! but I hope that your feeling
much better darling, and that it is nothing serious.

I can hardly wait till you get here
on Wednesday, I miss you so very much,
and I'm looking forward to phoning you to-nite
It always makes me feel real good when I talk
to you. I love you so very very much.

Well darling there's not much
more to say now, my Regards to Dr & Jo
+   All my love — Always & Forever
                                    Rudi.

Future Plans: November

As soon as we were engaged we started making plans for our future, even though we had not yet set the wedding date.

My parents home would be our home base and a hotel in Pittsburgh, our favorite city, an occasional base. Many of my friends would still be there and we wanted to stay in contact. Although we were staunch Catholics and wanted a family, we agreed to wait two or three years, so I could travel. Rudi was very adamant he wanted me with him and I certainly wanted to be with him.

Showboat: December 1954

Rudi and I were together in Lorain, Ohio. The Crew-Cuts were appearing there at the Showboat, where they were always a big hit. With family and friends, we were celebrating my twenty-second birthday. They sang "Happy Birthday" to me as everybody joined in. It was a party to remember.

The Crew-Cuts were now number one in the country, so very popular. Soon they'd be on their way to New York to appear on television; the Eddie Fisher Show, Perry Como, and the Ed Sullivan Show, where they performed one of my favorite songs, "Dance, Mr. Snowman." Their next appearance was to be back at the Copa in Pittsburgh for a very nostalgic week.

A few times, Rudi was able to meet me as I finished work. He would come up to the floor early and would visit with some of the patients that wanted to meet him. He enjoyed doing this and the patients were thrilled.

The Copa was so special for me; it had all started there almost eight months ago. My roommates and many of the other nurses were planning to be there every night. I'd bought a stunning red dress for the holidays, which I wore opening night. A table was reserved for us all week. That first night (the club was sold out every night) midway through the show, unbeknownst to me Rudi announced our engagement and asked me to stand. Feeling so proud, I stood and happily gave a wave. What a wonderful show, and as usual the Pittsburgh audiences were the greatest!

The next day the D.J.s were talking about the engagement. As one of them put it, "…and now there were only three available Crew-Cuts."

A few days later, I got my second phone call from the administrator's office at the hospital. The newspapers had been calling all morning, begging for interviews. The administrator said it was up to me, and they would allow me to give one or two interviews, and even have a few pictures taken at the hospitals. I was very surprised.

So I said "yes" and, in full uniform, I was photographed. I didn't realize this would be on the front page. I didn't like the picture.

Near the end of December, the Crew-Cuts were going home to Toronto.

Engagement Of Placeda Dee Conteen
And Rudi Maugeri Announced

Canadian's Fiancee

Prospective Bridegroor
Member Of The Crew-
Well Known Vocal Qu

Miss Conteen Is Member Of Nursi
At Allegheny General Hospital; Gr
From North Union High School; N

Mrs. Charles Dzamba, rear 120 East Ma
announcing the engagement of her daughter
Conteen, to Rudi Maugeri, son of Mr. and
Maugeri, Toronto, Ontario, Canada.

Miss Conteen is an alumna of North Uni
high school, Class of 1951, and is a member of
staff at the Allegheny General
hospital, Pittsburgh. She gradu
ated from that hospital's School
of Nursing in 1954.

Her fiance graduated from St.
Michael's Choir school, Toronto,
with the Class of 1946. He is a
member of the well known vocal
quartet, the Crew-Cuts, Mercury
recording artists.

No wedding date has been re-
vealed by the couple.

The Uniontown
Evening Standard

Placeda Dee Conteen, daughter of Mrs. Charles
Dzamba, of rear 120 East Main street, is the bride-elect of
Rudi Maugeri, son of Mr. and Mrs. Frank Maugeri,
Toronto, Canada. The couple has not selected a wedding
date.

Pittsburgh Sun-Telegraph

Roun............. 23
Social............. 11
George............. 13
George.............
Radio.......... by 8
Kenneti............. 23
Sports............. 8
Theaters............. 14, 15
TV Topic............. 6, 7
Wishing............. 23
Walter V............. 22
Women's............. 9
.... 21, 22

Only Pi..
using both
and Intern.
oad, pi.

newspaper
ted Press
ews wire
vice.

WEDNESDAY, DECEMBER 22, 1954

Recording Leads to Romance

A former Miss Uniontown,
now a nurse at Allegheny General Hospital, today admitted
that she's engaged to Rudi Maugeri, a member of the "Crew
Cuts" vocal quartet.

Nurse Placeda Dee Conteen,
22, taking time from her nursing duties for a hasty interview, said the song "Crazy 'bout
You, Baby" started the romance. Maugeri wrote the music for the tune.

She was so "crazy" about the
song that she spent her last two
dollars on a shopping spree just
Easter for a recording of it—

leaving her no money to go
home to Uniontown for the
holiday. But with her record
for companionship, the then
student nurse Conteen admitted
she had a pleasant Easter.

Miss Uniontown of 1951,
Nurse Conteen placed third in
the contest for Miss Pennsylvania that year. She said
friends arranged an interview
with Maugeri when he was in
town last Fall.

First it was an autograph,
then letters—and well, she said,
you know the course of true
love.

In September, Miss Conteen
was graduated from nursing
school.

She's a 1951 graduate of
North Union High School in
Uniontown.

The wedding date is "in-
definite," Nurse Conteen said,
adding:

"The springtime might be
it."

She expects to visit with
Maugeri's family, the Frank
Maugeris, in Toronto, Ont.,
Canada, over the New Year
holiday.

Champion Musical Booked In Harris

By KARL KRUG

Notes From a Frayed Cuff

MARGE and Gower Champion, who'll reach Syria Mosque Jan. 28 in Paul Gregory's "3 for Tonight," are also co-starred with Betty Grable and Jack Lemmon in Columbia's CinemaScope-color musical, "Three for the Show," which has an early 1955 date—perhaps while the Champions are at the Mosque—in the J. P. Harris.

Forecast in this pillar the other day that "The Women" would be staged in the Playhouse has now been made official. It opens Feb. 3 in the Craft Avenue Theater . . . In addition to the balloon hoopla it will set off in the Gateway tomorrow, the International Theater will stage a motorcade procession from the same spot next Tuesday night prior to the ballet premiere in the Crafton Heights house.

Laurence Harvey, 25 years old, snared by Hollywood as soon as he completed "Romeo and Juliet," which opens the

LAURENCE HARVEY
.. youngest "Romeo" ..

new Guild Theater on Christmas Day, is the youngest Romeo in screen annals. Three other Romeos of film note — the late Leslie Howard, Francis X. Bushman and Harry Hilliard— were edging middle age when they shinnied up Juliet's balcony.

* * *

PLACEDA DEE CONTEEN, a former Miss Uniontown, and now a nurse at the Allegheny General Hospital, and Rudi Maugert of Toronto, Canada, are going to get married. Bridegroom-to-be is a member of that celebrated quartet, the Crew Cuts, who record for Mercury. No date has been set for the wedding.

Johnny Vass' outfit plays the Uniontown Country Club's Christmas dance for the fifth straight year tonight. They'll also repeat for the same spot's New Years Eve affair . . . Stanley-Warner boss M. A. Silver will host his annual Yule party for local Film Row branch managers tomorrow afternoon in the Clark Bldg.

Nicest Christmas present 20th Century-Fox sales exec C. C. Kellenberg received was the release of his Ruth from Shadyside Hospital, where she her been a patient with an infected knee . . . Blanche W. McNutt of the Harris circuit, is having a birthday . . . Bill Artzberger, of WDTV, will have one tomorrow.

* * *

JOHN BERTERA, the Horizon Room boniface, broke ground last Friday for the $750,000 restaurant-night-club he will build on the new Parkway . . . Jeannette Subsaro of the William Penn Hotel staff, and her husband, John, are departing by air for Miami where they'll spend Christmas and New Years.

Sylvia Goldman of the Stanley-Warner office, has gone to Mt. Vernon, N. Y., where she'll holiday with the Ben Kalmensons and attend the wedding tomorrow of her nephew, Howard, to New Rochelle's Lillie Rose Brunner, in the Ambassador Hotel. Miss Goldman is a sister of Mr. Kalmenson, for-

The Engagement coverage continues.

On Broadway

By DOROTHY KILGALLEN

FRED STRAUSS, manager of the Crew Cuts, just insured the vocal chords of his four shboomers for $100,000. . . . Strollers in the Times Square area wonder why no picture of Judy's face decorates the marquees for "A Star Is Born." . . . Those jumbo smiles around Tin Pan Alley are the result of the latest ASCAP dividends. The songwriters' checks are running 20 per cent higher than last year.

★ ★ ★

Maggie McNamara, who was so cute in "Three Coins in the Fountain," is heartbroken over the latest snag in her career. She set her sights on a big part in a Hollywood flicker, spent $1,000 on dramatic coaching for the role, then flunked the test.

Miss Kilgallen

★ ★ ★

AVA GARDNER'S recent admirer, bull fighter Luis Dominguin, tangled with Edward Bannion, a N. Y. business man, in a Paris nightclub. The old story: Bannion didn't like it when Luis made bull's eyes at his girl. . . . The season's hottest undercover romance stars a handsome—but not famous—actor and the wife of a dancing movie star.

★ ★ ★

New York's book-making fraternities are passing around the word that Miami Beach and other Florida pleasure districts will "get the okay" for more-or-less open gambling just in time for the Winter tourist trade.

★ ★ ★

HOLLYWOOD'S PREOCCUPATION with on-the-spot backgrounds for provincial pictures received a discouraging setback when frightful weather in Vermont sent Alfred Hitchcock's company for "The Trouble With Harry" trouping back to the West Coast where the sun shines on the salt boxes.

★ ★ ★

Now it appears certain that most of the "authentic" New England scenery in the film will be photographed in California, and reels and reels of genuine background footage will be thrown away.

★ ★ ★

ONE OF BRITAIN'S BEST ACTORS lost a week-end in P. J. Clarke's 3rd Avenue pub. . . . Composer Vernon Duke is 30 pounds lighter after a month on dried fruits and yogurt. . . . Out in Hollywood the very newest is toreador pants for men. (Bully!) . . .

★ ★ ★

The Ingrid Bergman-George Sanders movie, which was so long in the making, finally has been released in Italy—to ghastly notices. The critics put most of the blame on Rossellini's torpid direction. . . . The Eartha Kitt play, "Mrs. Patterson," is on a diet. Ten minutes lopped off already, more to go before it's in shape for Broadway.

$100,000 Voices

PHONE:
CH. 1-3713
CH. 1-2537

Fred Strauss Agency
SUITE 1008 HIPPODROME BUILDING
CLEVELAND 14, OHIO

My Dearest Pau;

Well darling it was real wonderful talking to you last nite. It made me feel a lot better. I was feeling kind of low & lonely & I just had to call. I knew you'd cheer me up. and believe me I felt real terrific when I finished talking to you. You made me feel real great. Wow, I'll ever love you. Your real wonderful.

I'm sending those cards out to-day. I'll sent them "A.S.M.P." to make sure you get them before Christmas "All Righty", and I'll send the Card to them.

I can hardly wait till the 29th comes rolling along. I'm really looking forward to it, and I know you are to. We should both have a real wonderful time. We'll be able to be with each other for 5 days. I can't think of a better way of starting the

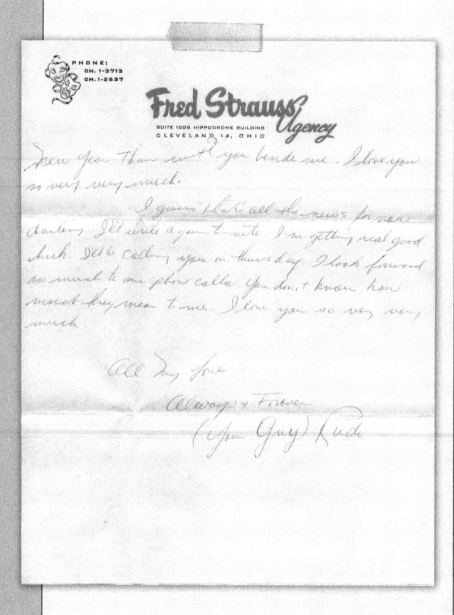

New Year than with you beside me. I love you
so very very much.

I guess that's all the news for now
darling. I'll write again to-nite. I'm getting real good
luck. I'll be calling you on thursday. I look forward
so much to our phone calls. You don't know how
much they mean to me. I love you so very very
much.

All My Love

Always & Forever

(Your Guy) Rudi

CHRISTMAS, 1954

On Christmas, my favorite holiday, I worked. I was happy to work because I was off to Toronto, Canada, for the New Year.

I left Wednesday, December 29th. I bought a beautiful brown suit, with a turquoise blouse to match my new turquoise wrap coat. To complete the outfit, I got the highest pair of brown heels a person could wear without falling off of them or twisting an ankle.

I had nine days off, the longest time Rudi and I had ever had together. I was meeting his family for the first time. I took a cab from the airport to the Maugeri home, where his mom and dad and a few others greeted me. Rudi was unexpectedly delayed but soon rushed in, then whisked me off to the second show.

The Crew-Cuts were appearing at the Casino Theater. I wanted to sit in the audience instead of backstage, so I could see and appreciate what the audience would hear and see. The guys ran on the stage and the crowd went wild! Their opening song was "There's No Place like Home for the Holidays." It was a wow. The teenagers' screams were deafening and thrilling.

NEW YEAR'S EVE, 1954: TORONTO, CANADA

On the morning of New Year's Eve, we all had breakfast together at the hotel. We all were so very upbeat. A new year ahead, and the Crew-Cuts were booked for a long engagement in Vegas, then were going to L.A. to make a movie. Of course, the biggest event of the year, they all said, was the wedding, and they all toasted me with orange juice.

The whole day was so busy. Between shows, running to interviews with the boys, including me being interviewed on the radio with the four of them behind the interviewer trying to make me laugh. Rudi was nervous for me, but he had forgotten I had been interviewed many times before (yes, before him!).

Publicity started coming out about the engagement, even though we had been engaged since November 12th. There were items in Walter Winchell's and Dorothy Kilgallen's columns, and in every paper. Suddenly, I was signing autographs with the guys!

I was there for every show. Just as Rudi said, we had to cherish every moment together since we were apart so much. I would stand backstage, and sometimes sit in the audience, but today it was standing room only.

We all went to a party and a dance for a while. Midnight found the Crew-Cuts and me at Midnight Mass. I couldn't thank God enough, for at that moment I felt that I was not only the happiest, but also the luckiest, girl in the world.

Chapter Seven

WEDDING BELLS ARE GOING TO CHIME

CHAPTER 7: WEDDING BELLS ARE GOING TO CHIME

Toronto, 1955

*O*ne night, the Crew-Cuts and I walked out the stage door into a very large group of screaming fans. Johnnie, Pat and Ray started signing autographs. Rudi and I were holding hands, and I heard a few screams of "There she is!" I looked around and asked Rudi who they saw. He held my hand tighter and said, "Honey, it's you, they want your autograph." I heard some call "Plus!" and some others "Miss Conteen!" so we walked over to them.

I said, "I am not an entertainer, I'm a nurse."

"You're Rudi's girl!"

"Yes, she is," said Rudi.

"Can we have your autograph?" they wanted to know.

I smiled. "Yes, you can."

Lotta Dempsey of *The Globe* newspaper had interviewed Rudi and me. Some had heard my radio interview too. I was so thrilled and happily signed them all, as Rudi beamed.

Toronto, Canada

By Lotta Dempsey

PERSON TO PERSON

It's the sort of thing that happens in the movies.

You listen to your favorite record over and over, and then the man with the voice you can't get out of your dreams comes to town, and you go to hear him.

And first thing you know you're dating in that wonderful little Italian restaurant with the red checkered table cloth and the good spaghetti—and bingo! You're engaged.

It happened to pretty blond Placeda Dee Conteen, not so long ago. And that's how she happens to be with her favorite member of the Crew Cuts, here in Toronto this week.

The old boys of St. Michael's Cathedral Choir, who are bringing their now famous close harmony back to Toronto audiences this week, list as their baritone former Toronto school teacher Rudi Maugeri. And it's easy to imagine just how Rudi felt that evening in the Pittsburgh Copa Club when he saw Placeda—Plus, for short —and her big blue eyes looking adoringly up at the quartet, from a ringside table.

It just happened that a mutual friend was able to introduce them, and during the Pittsburgh engagement Rudi took the pretty nurse on as many dates as his and her heavy work schedules allowed.

Rudi sang his heart out—and Plus found it right on the doorstep of the apartment she shared with two other soon-to-be-graduated nurses from Allegheny General Hospital.

The nurse (now finished her course) is making her first visit to Toronto to meet the folks. Rudi is taking her around to the old school and to see all his buddies and their gals.

The date isn't set—but from the look in both their eyes it won't be long.

Rudi is still pretty moved by the fact that when she heard the first Crew Cut disc—Crazy Bout Your Baby—Plus stood torn in the music store as to whether to buy it and walk home, or to save her last pennies for the bus ride, and let the music go.

She bought the record—and that was her last walk home.

Nurse 'Crazy 'Bout Crew Cut'

Ex-Beauty Queen To Wed Member Of Quartet

A former Miss Uniontown, now a nurse at Allegheny General Hospital, today admitted that she's engaged to Rudi Maugeri, a member of the "Crew Cuts" vocal quartet.

Nurse Placeda Dee Conteen, 22, taking time from her nursing duties for a hasty interview, said the song "Crazy 'bout You, Baby" started the romance. Maugeri wrote the music for the tune.

She was so "crazy" about the song that she spent her last two dollars on a shopping spree last Easter for a recording of it—leaving her no money to go home to Uniontown for the holiday. But with her record for companionship, the then student nurse Conteen admitted she had a pleasant Easter.

COURSE OF LOVE

Miss Uniontown of 1951, Nurse Conteen placed third in the contest for Miss Pennsylvania that year. She said friends arranged an interview with Maugeri when he was in town last Fall.

First it was an autograph, then letters—and well, she said, you know the course of true love.

In September, Miss Conteen was graduated from nursing school.

She's a 1951 graduate of North Union High School in Uniontown.

The wedding date is "indefinite," Nurse Conteen said, adding:

"The springtime might be it."

She expects to visit with Maugeri's family, the Frank Maugeris, in Toronto, Ont., Canada, over the New Year holiday.

THAT'S MY BOY . . . Nurse Placeda Dee Conteen, of Allegheny General Hospital, points to Rudi Maugeri, a member of the "Crew Cuts," to whom she says she is engaged.

Sun-Telegraph Photo by Edwin J. Morgan

The Word is Out!

January 1955

I found Toronto a beautiful, big city and the people so kind and friendly. We visited family and friends, and I saw the famous St. Michael's Choir School.

Jo started keeping a diary in December. She said that, with so much going on and the publicity following the engagement, we needed more than one recorder of events.

I met the famous Jimmy Komack and he became a friend, and also David Carroll, the musical arranger and conductor, was so nice.

While in Toronto, the roommates and I called each other every other day. Everything that was happening was so exciting, and they were thrilled for me.

From Jo's Diary:

Plus thought it was the beginning of a terrific New Year. Publicity hit on the engagement. She was signing autographs, being interviewed. What a thrill! Plus had already hit Walter Winchell's column and radio show, a celebrity in our midst.

January 2nd Plus has the flu.

January 4th Emergency phone call, she wasn't coming back.

January 6th. The wanderer returned.

Rudi and I talked about eloping, but quickly decided it would be impossible now.

On Sunday, January 9th, Mo, Jo, Jay, and I went to Youngstown, Ohio to see the Crew-Cuts. We got there a couple of hours before the show and stayed a few hours after. We had so much fun, and they were all happy to see us. We got home early in the morning, just in time to sadly go to work.

The next day, Mo walked the floor with Russ, as my former roommate Les was in labor. Jo and I were working and kept running up to the labor room to see how she was doing. We were all there to welcome our new nephew, David.

On January 29th Jo and I went to our first bridal fashion show. I immediately found my beautiful gown, one I'd seen on the cover of one of the magazines. I watched the show, looked at other beautiful gowns and, afterwards, tried the stunning cover gown. That was it! We hadn't set the date yet, but we did know it would be this summer.

The Warwick
LOCUST STREET AT 17TH
Philadelphia

My Dearest Phis:

Well darling were now in Philadelphia, and believe me when I say I'm sure glad you came to Youngstown. It made me feel real good to see you even if it was only for a few hrs. I miss you so very very much, and I feel real lonely. I only have one consolation — that I have the most wonderful girl in the world and pretty soon were going to be to-gether always. I love you so very very much.

Love,

(2)

Opening nite here last nite
was fine, and Ko-Ko-Mo is going
real great here there's no competition
at all. We're having a little bit
of trouble with Earth Angel because
there's a local record here by a
local girl but eventually I'm pretty
sure we'll take over on that here
also.

I sure hope Mo, Jo & Jay
enjoyed themselves last Sunday
because all the boys were really
glad they came down, and believe
me everybody thinks your all
wonderful girls.

(3)

Well darling after the show
last nite we visited one disc jockey
here, and then went to bed. I got
up an hr ago and now were
going to see all the disc jockeys
I got up at 9.00 A.M. its now
about 10.00 and were just
leaving.

I can hardly wait till
I phone you to-nite. I love
you so very very much. I could
say this a million times and still
it wouldn't be enough.

(over)

(4)

Well I guess that's all for
now darling I'll write you
again to-morrow.

All My Love

Always & Forever

Your Guy

Bud

P.S My love to all the gang (tell
Mo I want an account of what's
she's doing on the record).

The Warwick

LOCUST STREET AT 17TH · PHILADELPHIA 3, PA. · PENNYPACKER 5-3800

TELETYPE PH 376

My Dearest Plus:

Well darling things are going real great here, and the record is being played to death. The jockeys are real good to us here. Although, I don't like the club here too well. It's a nice room, and the people are swell, the boss treats us real good, but there's just something about it that I don't like. It's not a homy or cozy room. It leaves you real cold.

It was real great talking to you last nite, and I can hardly wait till you come down to St. Louis to see you again. I miss you so very very much. Darling I wish you wouldn't go to see "Dicks" group with mo & Jo. I just don't think you should go, so please don't go. I'll explain to you why when I talk to you.

The Warwick

LOCUST STREET AT 17TH · PHILADELPHIA 3, PA. · PENNYPACKER 5-3800

(2)

TELETYPE PH 376

Hey honey how about a little letter
I've sent three out, and I haven't got
any from you. How about it - eh. Your
goofing, and I really look forward to your
letters. I know your real busy & tired, but even if
it's just a few lines.

Darling I'm real miserable and
I miss you so very very much, and I can
hardly wait till we can be together always.
I love you so very very much.

Well I guess that's all for now
I'll write again to-morrow, and I'll call
on thursday.

all my love
Always & Forever
Your guy
Rich.

My Dearest Plus

Well darling we are now in Louisville
Kentucky as you can see by the lettering at the top of
the page. We played the theatre here, and we got
real terrific crowds all day. the last show
was at 10.00 pm After that the Mercury man here
and ourselves went to see one d y. then had something to eat, got back at the hotel about 1.00 AM and
I'm now writing you.

We leave at 10.30 in the morning
for Fort Wayne Indiana, where we'll be tomorrow
nite. So far the tour has been pretty successful
I hope it stays this way.

By the way darling I haven't
mentioned yet that I love you so very very
much, and that I can hardly wait till I

the Brown hotel

Louisville 2, Kentucky   Broadway at Fourth Ave.

Call you again to-morrow. I wish we were
in St. Louis now because I want to see you so
badly. Honey I want to talk about our getting
married & the date. I want you to be with me
always. Oh I miss you so very very much.
I am praying & hoping for the day when we'll be
to-gether for always & ever.

I'm going to close now darling
I'm pretty tired & I'm going to get a bit of sleep. We
have to get up at 9:00 in the morning, and on our way
again. I'll try & write again to-morrow. If not the
next day for sure.

All My Love
Always & Forever (Your Guy)
Rudi

1-23

THE SHERATON HOTEL
CHICAGO 11, ILL.

My Dearest Plus:

Well darling I'm now in Chicago
and in about a hr. will be on our way to
Kenosha Wis. We got into Chicago here
about 4:00 o'clock. We left Ft Wayne right
after the dance. I went right to bed as soon
as I arrived and got up at about 12:00. Just
finished having breakfast by myself here
at the Hotel. All the rest of them went out
somewhere to eat.

I find that All I want now
darling is to be alone & think of you all
the time. Every spare minute I get, I get
away from the rest of the gang & think of
you & write to you, because that's the
only thing that makes me really

happy. Darling I could never stop loving you the way I do, and I can just picture how happy we'll be when we get married and we'll be together always. I love you so very very much.

Darling the tour is going pretty good, and it seems to be pretty successful. We're getting good crowds, and it's helping to break our record down through the South these personal appearances really help.

I hope everything is going great in Pittsburgh and that Mo & Jo are getting along fine, and darling I hope your feeling well & taking real good care of yourself because when you don't feel good I worry about you. I don't

THE SHERATON HOTEL
CHICAGO 11, ILL.

(3)

want you to neglect your health at anytime. It's bad enough that I have to sometime. All Righty!

Well darling that's it for now I'll be phoning you Tuesday and I'll try to write to-morrow again. I can hardly wait tel I see you in St. Louis.

All My Love
Always + Forever
Your Guy

Rudi

Hotel **WAUSAU**

WAUSAU, WISCONSIN

WALTER SCHROEDER, PRESIDENT

My Dearest Plus;

     Well darling we are now in "Wausau Wisc" and its a pretty nice little town. We are playing the "Grand" theatre here and were going to do four shows.

     Right now the time is 4:30 p.m. for you its 5:30 p.m. We drove all nite from "Oshkosh" (had the biggest crowd they've ever had at the ballroom about "1300" people) arrived here at about 4:30 A.M. slept till 1:00 pm visited a few radio stations

HOTEL ASTOR
MILWAUKEE, WIS.
HOTEL RETLAW
FOND DU LAC, WIS.

HOTEL LORAINE
MADISON, WIS.
HOTEL VINCENT
BENTON HARBOR, MICH.

HOTEL SCHROEDER
MILWAUKEE, WIS.

HOTEL NORTHLAND
GREEN BAY, WIS.
HOTEL CALUMET
FOND DU LAC, WIS.

HOTEL DULUTH
DULUTH, MINN.
HOTEL WAUSAU
WAUSAU, WIS.

and I'm now at the theatre getting
ready for the first show.

I can hardly wait till
I call you to-nite darling, and I'll
be real glad when this tour is
over and I can see you in St.
Louis. I miss you more now than
I ever did. and I love you more +
more each day. I love you so
very very much.

Darling the record is
going real great. On Ko Ko Mo we're
a head of "Como" and Earth Angel
is starting to really step out by

HOTEL ASTOR
MILWAUKEE, WIS.
HOTEL RETLAW
FOND DU LAC, WIS.

HOTEL LORAINE
MADISON, WIS.
HOTEL VINCENT
BENTON HARBOR, MICH.

HOTEL SCHROEDER
MILWAUKEE, WIS.

HOTEL NORTHLAND
GREEN BAY, WIS.
HOTEL CALUMET
FOND DU LAC, WIS.

HOTEL DULUTH
DULUTH, MINN.
HOTEL WAUSAU
WAUSAU, WIS.

(5

us, so maybe we'll get two tunes
on the hit parade.

I hope you feeling real
great darling, and please don't
work to bad, get a lot of rest
and take real good care of yourself.
I guess I'll close now darling. I'll
write again tomorrow.

All my love

Always & Forever

Your Guy

Rack.

HOTEL ASTOR
MILWAUKEE, WIS.
HOTEL RETLAW
FOND DU LAC, WIS.

HOTEL LORAINE
MADISON, WIS.
HOTEL VINCENT
BENTON HARBOR, MICH.

HOTEL SCHROEDER
MILWAUKEE, WIS.

HOTEL NORTHLAND
GREEN BAY, WIS.
HOTEL CALUMET
FOND DU LAC, WIS.

HOTEL DULUTH
DULUTH, MINN.
HOTEL WAUSAU
WAUSAU, WIS.

My Dearest Plus,

Well darling I'm now in
Rock Island Ill, which is actually
a suburb of Davenport, where I told
you we would be. We're working
the Auto Show here. We do three
shows to-day & four to-morrow. We
just finished our first show here
to-day. We'll be here for two days
then the McClure Sisters follow us
in.

We arrived here about 6.00
A.M. after driving all night from

JACOB HOFFMANN, PRESIDENT

HOTEL HOFFMANN
SOUTH BEND, IND.

HOTEL MICHIANA
SOUTH BEND, IND.

HOTEL FORT ARMSTRONG
ROCK ISLAND, ILL.

WHERE FRIENDLY SERVICE PREVAILS

Written At Hotel _____

(2

Marion, Iowa. We left there right
after the show last night. I slept
tel 1.00 pm. Got up, ate breakfast.
Then we had to go + do a few
desk jockey shows, and then we did
our first show at 4:30.

Down this way in what
is known as the "quad city" theres
four little cities bunched to-gether
Davenport, Rock Island, Moline +
another one, we are very popular,
Earth Angel is number 1, here
& KoKoMo is no 2 on their hit

JACOB HOFFMANN, PRESIDENT

MARJORIE KENADY, ASS'T TO PRESIDENT

HOTEL HOFFMANN
SOUTH BEND, IND.

HOTEL MICHIANA
SOUTH BEND, IND.

HOTEL EUGENE
MONROE, WIS.

HOTEL FORT ARMSTRONG
ROCK ISLAND, ILL.

WHERE FRIENDLY   SERVICE PREVAILS

Written At Hotel_____

hit parade, by the way Kokomo
is in the top twenty all ready beye
us it is No 19 nationally isn't
that great.

Honey I can hardly wait
till I call you after the next show
and believe me I'm all excited. I
really look forward to our phone
calls, & I can hardly wait till
you come to St. Louis. I miss
you so very very much. I don't
know what to do with myself
when your not around. I

(4)

love you so very very much.

Well darling I'm going to
grab a bite to eat now, and then
back to the Auditorium for another
show, and then back again after
the show to call you.

I'll write again to-morrow

All my love

Always + Forever
Your Gal,
Rudi

February 1955: St. Louis, Missouri

I arrived in St. Louis on a beautiful, sunny, cold day, and ran straight into the arms of my guy. We were looking forward to this trip so much. I had three and a half days off.

The Chase Hotel was great, and the room in which they were appearing was quite elegant.

We walked around the town window shopping, going in and out of some of the interesting looking shops. I saw a dress that I liked in one of the shop windows, so we went in. Rudi said to the clerk, "My fiancé would like to try on the dress that's in your window." It was a beautiful boutique where they brought the clothes out to you.

One of the salesgirls recognized Rudi – she had been to the show two nights before – so we became fast friends. I kept modeling outfits as he sat sipping coffee and watching. He insisted on buying me the dress that I liked the best, the one from the window.

I wore it that evening and felt very special. We had pictures taken at the club. We had been invited to a big party after the show, at the home of an executive from Budweiser. I was invited to sit at the long table with the young people (my age) who would be at the party. I found some of them nice, but some of them were very impressed with themselves.

As the Crew-Cuts left the stage after their performance, I was surprised but pleased when one of the fellows at the table asked to look at my engagement ring. I offered him my hand for inspection, and he kind of sneered and said, "He's a Crew-Cut, and you got a small ring like that?"

I quickly pulled my hand back, looked at the little bastard and said, "I picked out this ring. I could have had any ring I wanted, but

I love this one, but more importantly, I love the person who gave it to me."

Rudi walked to the table, receiving many compliments from the group. He got to me and gave me a kiss on the cheek. I jumped up and said, "Let's dance."

I suggested to Rudi that maybe we could miss the party. He asked what was wrong; I had been so excited to go. I agreed to go, since the plans had been made.

I did tell him afterwards about the ring. He was sorry that someone would be that rude to me. I told him what I'd said to the jerk. We both said at the same time, "Let's forget it. Our time together is too short to let anyone or anything upset it." I forgot all about it but, as it turned out, Rudi certainly didn't.

On the way to the airport Rudi asked me to set the date. I chose August the sixth. On Sunday I left St. Louis at 11 in the morning. I told the stewardess not to bring me a meal, and fell asleep as the plane was taking off. The next thing I heard was the captain announcing we would be landing in New York. I thought for a panicked moment that I'd somehow slept through the Pittsburg stop – but wait, I was on a plane, not a train. It turned out that the Pittsburgh airport was fogged in. In order to get these three and a half days off, I had promised to be back in time to work Sunday night. Now I couldn't get back until Monday morning.

When Rudi called Sunday evening and Mo told him I was stuck in New York, he couldn't believe it. He told her we had set a date and now he couldn't just let me wander around alone on these trips. We were going to be together forever.

My mother, my godmother Marie, and I went to a bridal fashion show and found gowns for the bridesmaids and the flower girl. We girls stayed up all night making wedding plans.

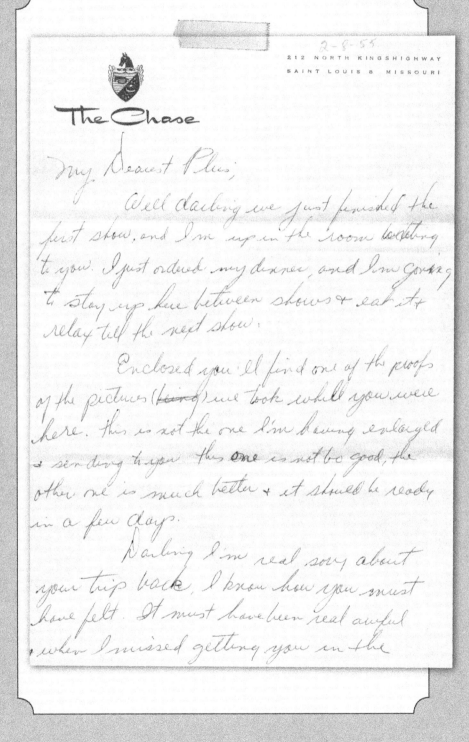

The Chase

My Dearest Plus;

Well darling we just finished the first show, and I'm up in the room talking to you. I just ordered my dinner, and I'm going to stay up here between shows & eat it & relax till the next show.

Enclosed you'll find one of the proofs of the pictures (~~thing~~) we took while you were here. this is not the one I'm having enlarged & sending to you this one is not too good, the other one is much better & it should be ready in a few days.

Darling I'm real sorry about your trip back, I know how you must have felt. It must have been real awful when I missed getting you in the

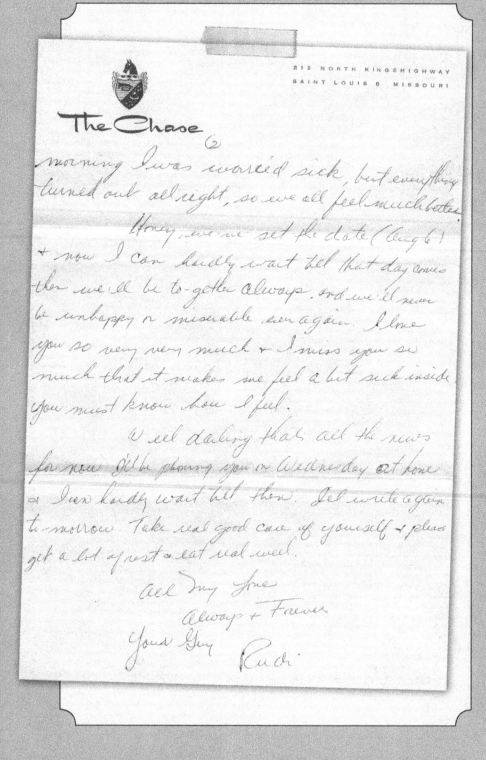

morning I was worried sick, but everything turned out all right, so we all feel much better.

Honey, we've set the date (Aug 6) & now I can hardly wait till that day comes then we'll be together always, and we'll never be unhappy or miserable ever again. I love you so very very much & I miss you so much that it makes me feel a bit sick inside you must know how I feel.

Well darling that's all the news for now. I'll be phoning you on Wednesday at home & I can hardly wait till then. I'll write again to-morrow. Take real good care of yourself & please get a lot of rest & eat real well.

All My Love
Always + Forever
Your Guy

Rudi

212 NORTH KINGSHIGHWAY
SAINT LOUIS 8 · MISSOURI

The Chase

My Dearest Plus;

Well darling Im in bed now writing this letter. We just finished the last show I went out & grabbed a bite to eat, and now I'm ready to get some sleep.

I feel pretty miserable without you darling. I just feel lost & I don't know what to do with myself. I think about you night & day & I can hardly wait till I phone you later on to-day. Lets see in about 16 hrs (Its now 2.30 Am. here) I'll be talking to you. I love you so very very much. Darling you don't know just how much I miss you.

Guess what I took my ring to get it fixed yesterday & It'll be ready to-day. Pretty good huh!

Got the new billboard to-day. Ko KoMo is No 8 & Earth Angel is No 9 nationally. Comes

212 NORTH KINGSHIGHWAY
SAINT LOUIS 8 MISSOURI

The Chase ②

is still a bit ahead of us on sales, but we moved up about six spots on the charts & the only moved up one - I'd say within 2 or 3 weeks we should be ahead of him.

Well that's all the news for now darling. I'll write again tomorrow & until I phone you.

All my Love
Always & Forever
Your Guy (Rudi)

P.S. Excuse the writing luck. As you know I'm writing this in bed

Love You Always
Rudi

The Chase

My Dearest Plus;

My darling it was real
wonderful talking to you last nite, although
at times I didn't show it, but I got that
way because I miss you so much honey.
You just can't realize how I feel about
you. I'm always in a trance thinking of
you all the time. I love you so very very
much.

I'm in bed writing this letter again.
We finished the last show a short while ago.
I went out & had a bite to eat with Harry
Fender the disc jockey here at the hotel. Remember
we were on his show in the small room
at the side. It was very interesting talking to
him because he use to be on broadway at

The Chase

(2)

one time, and Al Jolson, Eddie Cantor &
all those old stars were his best friends &
he was telling me all about them.

I have to get up at 9:00 o'clock
to-morrow morning, we have to visit a
few record stores, and also do a few dise
jockeys & make a personal appearance at the
big department store here to-morrow afternoon
So we've got a pretty busy day ahead of us.

Well darling its about 2:30
AM and I think I'll get some sleep. I'll write
again to-morrow. I'll be calling you on Friday
So until then

All My Love
Always & Forever

(Your Guy) Rudi

P.S. I hope Jo is feeling a lot better

The Chase

My Dearest Plus

Well darling its Saturday + things have been going pretty good down here. Our Ko Ko Mo is now No 1. here so that makes us feel pretty good + Earth Angel is about 4 or 5.

Darling why I've been sounding a bit discouraged over the phone these last few days is because, I feel real lonely + miss you so very very much. In fact I felt real miserable, and then when I talk to you over the phone I wish so badly that I could be with you that it really hurt me inside I love you so very very much. I'm real sorry if I make you feel bad when I'm like this. I'll try not + be like that anymore. What a character I am, huh! I don't know how you put up with me.

The Chase (2)

Darling Dear hardly wait till
I see you on the 22nd. It'll be just wonderful
I hope everything is going great in Pittsburgh
and I'm real sorry to hear about Jo. I hope
its nothing too serious & that she gets better
real fast.

Last nite after I called you I got
ready for the show & we had a pretty good
nite at the Club despite the fact it was
about 5 below zero here. After the last show
I went & had something to eat with Pat
& then went to bed about 2.30. We were up
at 8.30 to do the "Ed Bonner" show then we
got something to eat did another disc jockey
show, and now were resting a bit before
we do "Saturday afternoon at the Chase" show
here.

Well that's the news up to now
honey. I'll be calling you to-morrow

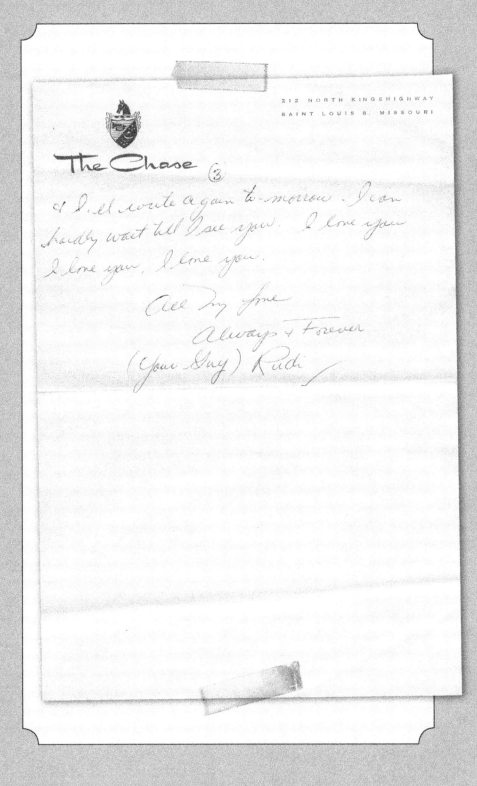

The Chase ③

& I'll write again to-morrow. I can
hardly wait till I see you. I love you
I love you, I love you.

All My Love
Always + Forever
(Your Guy) Rudi

212 NORTH KINGSHIGHWAY
SAINT LOUIS 8, MISSOURI

The Chase

My Dearest Plus:

Well darling, it was wonderful
talking to you to-nite. It made me feel
real-woonderful, now I can go to sleep
& dream about you, I love you so
very very much.

Everything is going real great
here & we we had a real woonderful
engagement, everybody seems real pleased.
So that is something to feel happy about
We are leaving to-morrow morning early
we'll be in Springfield Ill. to-morrow
then on Thursday we'll be in Urbano Ill.
that's when I'll be phoning you

how are things going in Pittsburg
for us, they playing our records here, Kokomo

The Chase ③

is showing real great on the charts there, so I guess the d j's are doing a good job for us there.

Well honey there's not much more to say & I'm pretty tired. I love you, I love you, I love you.

All My Love
Always & Forever
(Your Guy) Rudi

P.S. Hope Jo's operation turns out okay, tell her I was asking about her, and I hope she's up & around real fast.

At The Chase in St. Louis.

This is the dress that Rudi bought for me.

On the 18th of February, Rudi called with very big news; a possible contract to take the group to England. We moved the wedding date to June 4th, since he wanted me with him and we could have a European honeymoon.

Jo wrote in the diary:

February 21st, Monday; Mo and Plus bustled around cleaning house and shopping. Happy day. Rudi was coming home! On Tuesday at 4:30 P.M. the phone call, Rudi was at the airport. Plus made dinner for him and Mo.

The next day Rudi and Plus took Uniontown by storm. Went to church, found out that June 4th was already taken, so June 11th was definitely set with the church and hotel etc.

Diamond Lil, that's what we call her. Yes, she got another ring from Rudi – what a rock!! Wedding bands were picked out and formal publicity pictures taken. Friday, back to Pittsburgh, and a group of us got decked out and went out to dinner and dancing at two of our favorite places to celebrate. We had a ball!!

Saturday, Plus tearfully saw Rudi off to the plane. She had never cried before when leaving him but he was off to Las Vegas and Hollywood and, with making all the wedding arrangements in Uniontown and working in Pittsburgh, they would not be seeing each other for five weeks, not until April in Chicago.

Wedding Plans Are Revealed By
Bride-Elect, Placeda Dee Conteen

St. Mary's Church To Be Setting For Marriage To Rudi Maugeri Of Toronto

A pretty summer wedding which will be solemnized June 11 will be that of Placeda Dee Conteen, daughter of Mrs. Charles Dzamba, 120 E. Main St., and Rudi Maugeri, son of Mr. and Mrs. Frank Maugeri of 13 Simpson Ave., Toronto, Canada.

St. Mary's R. C. Church will be the setting for the double ring ceremony at 10 o'clock with the Rev. Andrew Hredzak officiating. Mrs. Frances Wrable will provide traditional organ music. Dominic Maugeri and Mrs. Wrable will be soloists.

The prospective bride has asked Jo Ann Lazaran, 48 N. Gallatin Ave., to serve as maid of honor. Bridesmaids will be Mary Wallace of Beaver Falls; Ceatta O'Soka, cousin of the future bride, Windham, Ohio; Patricia Kelly, Cleveland, Ohio; and Margaret Schreckengost, an aunt, Lorain, Ohio. The bride-elect's cousin, little Mary Frances Cunningham of Lorain, will be flower girl.

Mr. Maugeri will be attended by his brother, Dr. George Maugeri of Toronto. Ushers will be Pat Barrett, Johnnie and Ray Perkins, all members of the well known vocal quartet, The Crew-Cuts, and their manager, Fred Strauss.

Miss Conteen graduated from North Union Twp. High School, class of 1951, and Allegheny General Hospital School of Nursing, class of 1954. She is now a member of the staff of that hospital in Pittsburgh.

Her fiance attended St. Michael's Choir School and University in Toronto and is a member of The Crew-Cuts, Mercury label recording artists.

The Wedding Plans make the paper too!

TWA
TRANS WORLD AIRLINES
in flight

My Dearest Plus,

Well darling guess where I'm writing this letter. I'm in a T W A plane 14,000 ft in the air, going about 215 m p h and still two hrs to go before we hit Los Angelos, Wow what a ride we've been in the air about 4 hrs already. I just found out to that the time change is 3 hrs difference now, when its 6.00 pm in Pgh, its only 3 pm here or I should say in L A.

Darling I miss you so very very very much, I can hardly wait till June 11 then we'll be together for always & ever. I'm never going to let you out of my sight for one second after were married, that to make up for the lost time when I'm away from you now. I love you so very very very much

Well the show at the ballroom was over about 12:30 last nite. After that I went & had something to eat at Eddy's where we played the last time we were there, and the owner said he wants to be invited to the wedding for sure, and he wants you to come down when we play there in May. I showed him your pictures & he thinks your real terrific. I left there about 1:30 then went right home to bed. Got up at 9:00 & went to Mass, got back about 10:30 had breakfast, checked out & went to the airport, the plane was late so we had to wait around till about 1:30 before we could get on, and then we were off.

As soon as we arrive in L.A. we have to go to the T.V. studio for rehearsal and then the show. So we're going to be pretty

TWA TRANS WORLD AIRLINES

in flight

3

busy, and from what I've heard there's a lot of desk jockey shows + personal appearance so these two days in L.A. are going to be pretty rough. We leave for Los Vegas Tuesday morning, and I'll be calling you Tues. evening.

Well darling that's all the news for now, I'll write again to-nite. Please take good care of yourself + eat real well, hnh, because I worry about you.

All My Love
Always + Forever
(Your Guy) Rudi

P.S. Give my regards to Mo + Jo.

March 1955: More Wedding Plans

Rudi had been gone about three days, and I missed him so much. Three months 'till the big day, such a daunting but exciting prospect.

There would be at least four hundred people at the wedding. Fred (the Crew-Cuts' manager) hadn't given Rudi the guest list yet, but I did know that there would be entertainers, disc jockeys, some club managers, and also family and friends from Canada.

The Morning Herald and *Evening Standard*, our local newspapers, *The Pittsburgh Post Gazette*, and even a Toronto paper, would all be covering our wedding.

Rudi had been in L.A. for two days rehearsing and doing a television show, then Wednesday, March 2nd, the Crew-Cuts opened at the El Rancho Vegas. Friday, they started taking dancing lessons, rehearsing a lot of new numbers for their floor show, and getting ready to record in another week. They were flying back and forth to L.A. for the movie. Starting to build the act, they had just hired a man from Hollywood to write special material. Their opening night was a tremendous success; they had to turn people away.

Mo, Jo, and I were trudging off in the cold to work the 11 P.M. to 7 A.M. shift. Jo and I went to the bridal shop, decided we definitely loved these bridesmaids' gowns and hats, and they were ordered.

My Aunt Mary brought her daughter, Mary Frances, in from Ohio. She was going to be my little flower girl and was so excited. P.K. came in from Ohio, along with my Aunt Margaret, to be fitted, and my cousin Ceatta. Mo, Jo and Les were my bridesmaids, of course. Each time someone would come for a fitting, the excitement level would go up. It was such a happy time!

Rudi asked if I could come out to Vegas for a weekend, please. On the phone we compared our busy schedules, and then agreed that no matter how much we missed each other, we would cross off the days on the calendar and be patient. We both wrote more letters and made more phone calls. He wrote twenty-one letters, and if he was too busy to write, then he was sure to call. I usually received calls on the same days I got letters.

I went home to find that our publicity engagement pictures were ready. As Jo wrote in her diary, "Wow!! Movie Stars!" I called Rudi immediately, so excited, to say that I'd bring them to Chicago in a couple weeks. But he couldn't wait to see them, so I had Spellman Photography Studio send them out that day. They were happy to oblige, since they were doing the wedding.

March was really moving along quickly, between trips back and forth to Uniontown, having gown fittings, writing invitations, choosing the menu and flowers, and arranging housing for out-of-towners. Rudi was sorry he couldn't help me with all of it, but knew that it would be a beautiful day.

Rudi called me twice on Sunday March 27th. He was very lonesome, he told me, and couldn't sleep all night, but it was only about two weeks until we would be together in Chicago. They finished their movie short. At this time "Don't Be Angry" came out, which was terrific. "Chop Chop Boom" was good, but not a favorite of mine. Rudi always said I could pick the winners! Their Vegas booking was extended a few more days, but now he was anxious to leave.

Official Engagement Photo for Publicity

My Dearest Plus,

Well darling its about 1:15 A.M.
here. we just finished our last d. j.
show, came right back to the hotel &
I'm in bed already. We had a real
long day. I've been up since 6:30 this
morning, and we've been going constantly
all day long. So I'm real tired

This is a beautiful part of the
country. It's like a little paradise. It's
very scenic, and everything seems so
clean & spotless. I wish you was here
with me to see it.

Darling right now I'd like
to mention that I love you, I love you
I love you I could say this for always
& ever, and each time I would mean it

2

more & more. Honey I hope these next
few months really fly. I want you to
be with me for always & a day.

Guess what, honey, we'll only
be down the coast here for 5 weeks. Plans
have changed a bit, then we come back
East to the Chicago theatre for three weeks
So that's real good news.

We catch a 9:40 plane to-morrow
for Vegas, and rehearsal start at 12 noon
So I guess to-morrow we'll be another busy
day.

Well I guess that's all the news
for now darling thinking of you always.
I'll write again when soon we get to Vegas.

All My Love
Always & Forever
Your Guy Rudi

My Dearest Phu,

312

Darling please excuse
the paper. I just got back from
doing the last show + found
out we had no writing paper
left, and its kind of late to
get some now, but I ~~wanted to~~
wanted to write you now +
not wait till to-morrow so I
made something to write on
out of envelopes. Pretty cute,
huh!

It was real wonderful
talking to you at dinnertime
It made me feel so good.
But honestly honey it really
worries me when you sound
a little sad, and you seemed
to sound that way to-nite. I
know its hard being away
from each other, and believe me
darling I feel exactly the same
way you do, but its only a
little while longer and you

we'll always be to-gether. Darling I love you so very very much, and darling I'm sorry about going out with the guys the other nite, but I promise I won't do it again. I don't want you to do it, therefore I won't do it either. If I had known I'd be hurting you + thought a little more I wouldn't have gone. I'm real sorry. It won't ever happen again. Anyway I'm just satisfied coming straight to bed + thinking of you. I love you so very very much.

The opening show went real great + they had to turn people away it was so jammed. Let's hope it stays like that.

Well darling that's all for now. When I call you on Saturday I'll tell you the exact date we open in Chicago so you can make arrangements to come down.

All my love always + forever Your Guy) Rudi

HOTEL
El Rancho Vegas

ON HIGHWAY 91 - LAS VEGAS, NEVADA

My Dearest Plus;

Well darling another day is over & another day closer to our wedding. We finished the last show at about 12:30, then we went to see a disc jockey, had a bite to eat, came back to our rooms & now I'm writing you.

We moved from our other rooms here & the owner here gave us a wonderful little cottage. It got four rooms; two rooms with twin beds, for us guys a single room for Fred & a living room. It real cute

Hney Fred's keeping us real busy to-morrow we start taking dancing lessons, from this guy down here who's suppose to be pretty good & besides that

AMERICA'S FINEST WESTERN HOTEL

were rehearsing a lot of new numbers for our floor show + getting ready for our record session, Dave is coming down in about a week to record. I have to get up about 9 o'clock. I have so much work ahead of me that I don't know where to start. We're really starting to build our act. To-day we just hired a guy from Hollywood to write special material for our act. So we should come up with something real great, I hope.

the show is going real tremendous here they've had to turn people away every nite so far. It looks like we've got the best show down here. Let's hope it stays that way.

Darling I can hardly wait to call you

(3)

on Saturday evening. I miss you more + more each day.
I'm so very very happy that we're getting married in
June. I don't think I could possibly wait any longer.
It's killing me to wait even till June. All I look forward
to from day to day is our marriage. I love you. I love you.
I love you.

        Darling that's all the news for now. I'll write
again tomorrow, and I'll be phoning you on Saturday.

            All My Love
            Always + Forever
    (Your Guy) Kath

My Dearest Rhea,

Well darling it was real wonderful talking
to you this afternoon. I wish I could have talked a
lot longer, but I'll make up for that to-morrow
nite when I call you.

Well to-morrow we go to L.A. to start
making the movie short for Universal Pictures.
Bill Haley is also going to be in it. We have to
go in To-morrow & then Monday again. Boy
if we don't stop rehearsing & running around
so much. I feel like I could rest for a couple
of weeks with no trouble at all.

I hope that your feeling real great

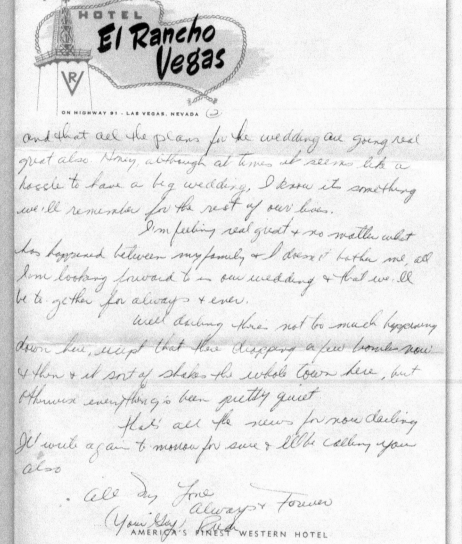

and that all the plans for the wedding are going real great also. Honey, although at times it seems like a hassle to have a big wedding, I know its something we'll remember for the rest of our lives.

I'm feeling real great & no matter what has happened between my family & I doesn't bother me. all I'm looking forward to is our wedding & that we'll be together for always & ever.

Well darling there's not to much happening down here, except that there dropping a few bombs now & then & it sort of shakes the whole town here, but otherwise everything's been pretty quiet.

That's all the news for now darling I'll write again tomorrow for sure & I'll be calling you also

All my Love
Always & Forever
(Your Guy), Rich

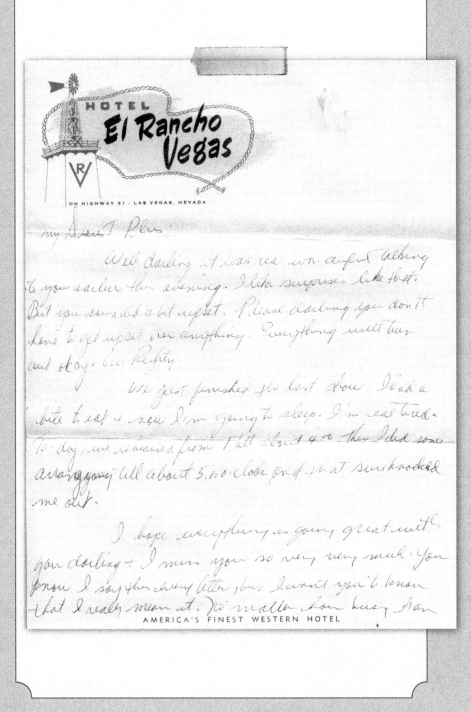

HOTEL
El Rancho Vegas

ON HIGHWAY 91 - LAS VEGAS, NEVADA

My dearest Plus,

Well darling it was real won aful talking
to you earlier this evening. I like surprise like that.
But you sounded a bit upset. Please darling you don't
have to get upset over anything. Everything will turn
out okay. Our Rarity.

We just finished the last show. I had a
bite to eat + now I'm going to sleep. I'm real tired.
To-day we rehearsed from 1 till about 4.00 then I did some
arranging till about 5.00 o'clock and that sure knocked
me out.

I hope everything is going great with
you darling + I miss you so very very much. You
know I say this every letter, but I want you to know
that I really mean it. No matter how busy I am

AMERICA'S FINEST WESTERN HOTEL

(2)

I still miss you more than anybody could miss
the girl they love. Oh darling I love you, I love
you, I love you. I could say this every second of
the day & I would never get tired.

　　　Well I think I'll close now, I'll write
again to-morrow, and I'll be phoning you to-nite.
So till then

　　　　　　　All my love
　　　　　　　　Always & Forever
　　　(Your Guy) Rudi

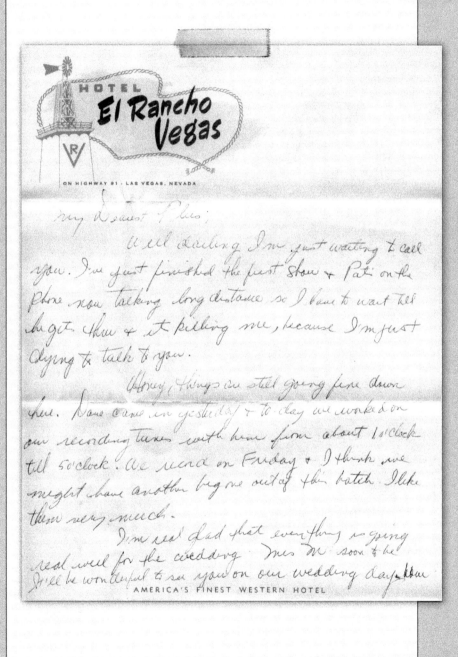

My Dearest Plus;

Well darling I'm just waiting to call you. I've just finished the first show & Pati on the phone now talking long distance so I have to wait till she get thru & it killing me, because I'm just dying to talk to you.

Honey, things are still going fine down here. Dave came in yesterday & today we worked on our recording tunes with him from about 1 o'clock till 5 o'clock. We record on Friday & I think we might have another big one out of this batch. I like them very much.

I'm real glad that everything is going real well for the wedding. Mrs. M. soon to be. It will be wonderful to see you on our wedding day. Hon

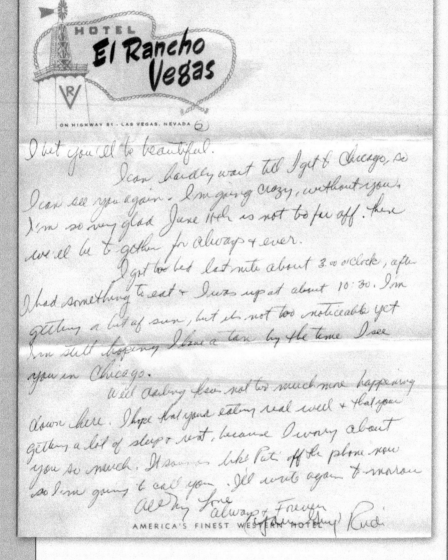

HOTEL
El Rancho Vegas

ON HIGHWAY 91 · LAS VEGAS, NEVADA

I bet you'll be beautiful.

I can hardly wait till I get to Chicago, so I can see you again. I'm going crazy, without you. I'm so very glad June 16th is not too far off. There we'll be together for always & ever.

I got to bed last nite about 3:00 o'clock, after I had something to eat & I was up at about 10:30. I'm getting a bit of sun, but it's not too noticeable yet. I'm still hoping I have a tan by the time I see you in Chicago.

Well darling there's not too much more happening down here. I hope that your eating real well & that your getting a lot of sleep & rest, because I worry about you so much. It sounds like Pat off the phone now so I'm going to call you. I'll write again tomorow.

All My Love
Always & Forever
Rudi

AMERICA'S FINEST WESTERN HOTEL

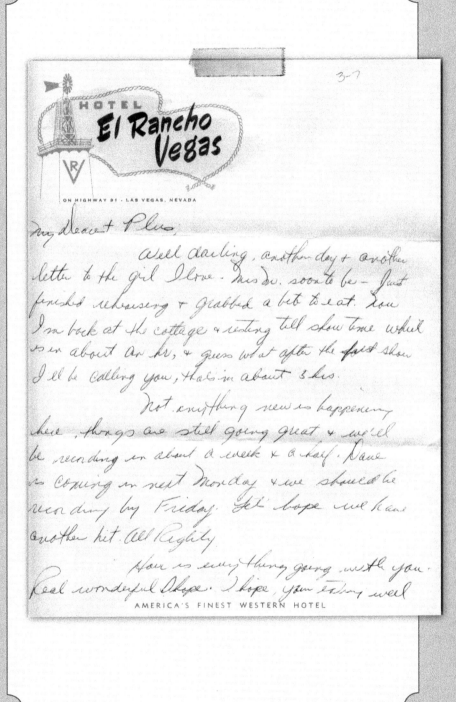

HOTEL
El Rancho Vegas

ON HIGHWAY 91 · LAS VEGAS, NEVADA

My Dearest Plus,

      Well darling, another day & another letter to the girl I love. Mrs. soon to be — Just finished rehearsing & grabbed a bite to eat. Now I'm back at the cottage & resting till show time which is in about an hr., & guess what after the first show I'll be calling you, that's in about 3 hrs.

      Not anything new is happening here, things are still going great & we'll be recording in about a week & a half. Dave is coming in next Monday & we should be recording by Friday. Let's hope we have another hit. All Righty.

      How is everything going with you. Real wonderful I hope. I hope you eating well

AMERICA'S FINEST WESTERN HOTEL

& getting a lot of rest, and that your taking things
real easy. If you do, you'll find out that you'll feel
a lot happier.

     I'm thinking about you nite & day darling
and I have a pretty empty feeling inside of me
whenever I'm away from you, but I'm always
thinking when I'll see you again & then when will
be to-gether for always & ever. I love you so
very very much.

     I'll close for now, darling

All My Love
    Always & Forever
(Your Guy) Rudi

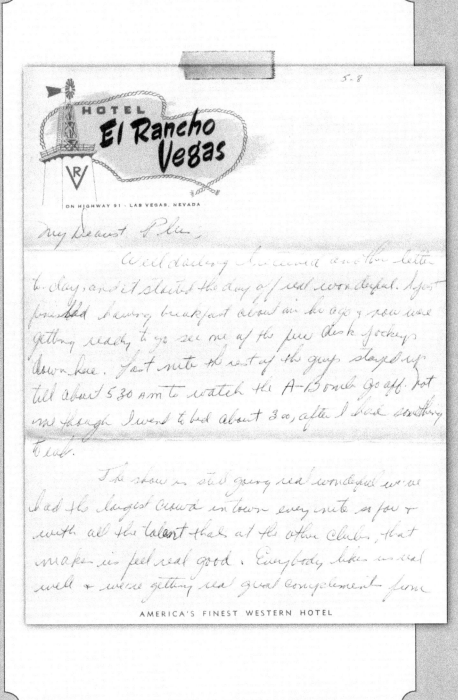

HOTEL
El Rancho
Vegas

ON HIGHWAY 91 · LAS VEGAS, NEVADA

My Dearest Plu,

Well darling I received another letter
to day, and it started the day off real wonderful. I just
finished having breakfast about an hr ago & now were
getting ready to go see one of the free desk jockeys
down here. Last nite the rest of the guys stayed up
till about 5 30 am to watch the A-Bomb go off. Not
me though I went to bed about 3 00, after I had something
to eat.

The show is still going real wonderful we've
had the largest crowd in town every nite so far &
with all the talent that at the other clubs, that
makes us feel real good. Everybody likes us real
well & were getting real great compliments from

AMERICA'S FINEST WESTERN HOTEL

everybody so that makes us feel real good.

Dave is coming down on the 14th to start our recording sessions & we're going to record all that week, by the time we get to Chicago we should have another record out. We haven't any idea what we're recording for our pop release at all, but I hope it's something real great.

I hope your feeling well & eating real great & remember what I told you that Jo's in the hospital again, if you ever need any help financially you'd better ask me, or I'll get mad. All Righty?

Darling I miss you so very very much I've been getting so lonely these last few days that I just don't know what to do with myself, but It won't be long now when we'll be together for

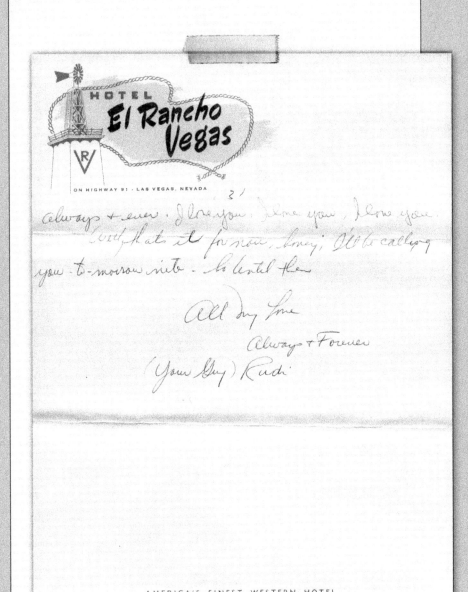

HOTEL

El Rancho Vegas

ON HIGHWAY 91 · LAS VEGAS, NEVADA

always + ever. I love you, I love you, I love you.
Well that's it for now, honey; I'll be calling
you to-morrow nite. So until then

All my love
Always + Forever
(Your Guy) Rudi

AMERICA'S FINEST WESTERN HOTEL

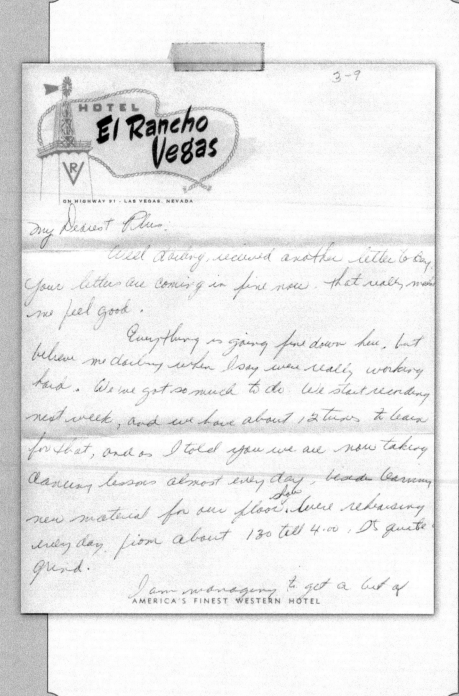

HOTEL
El Rancho
Vegas

ON HIGHWAY 91 · LAS VEGAS, NEVADA

My Dearest Plus;

Well darling, received another letter to day,
your letters are coming in fine now. that really makes
me feel good.

Everything is going fine down here, but
believe me darling when I say were really working
hard. We've got so much to do. We start recording
next week, and we have about 12 tunes to learn
for that, and as I told you we are now taking
dancing lessons almost every day, beside learning
new material for our floor show. were rehearsing
every day, from about 130 till 4.00. It's quite a
grind.

I am managing to get a bet of

AMERICA'S FINEST WESTERN HOTEL

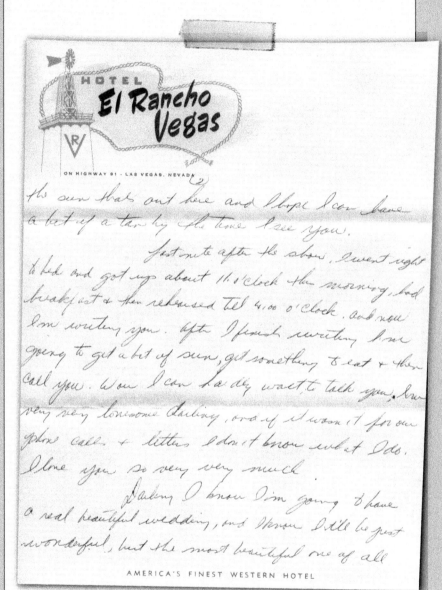

HOTEL
El Rancho
Vegas

ON HIGHWAY 91 · LAS VEGAS, NEVADA

the sun that out here and I hope I can have
a bit of a tan by the time I see you.

Last nite after the show, I went right
to bed and got up about 11 o'clock this morning, had
breakfast & then rehearsed till 4.00 o'clock. And now
I'm writing you. After I finish writing I'm
going to get a bit of sun, get something to eat & then
call you. Wow I can hardly wait to talk you, I'm
very very lonesome darling, and if it wasn't for our
phone calls & letters I don't know what I'd do.
I love you so very very much.

Darling I know I'm going to have
a real beautiful wedding, and I know it'll be just
wonderful, but the most beautiful one of all

HOTEL El Rancho Vegas

ON HIGHWAY 91 · LAS VEGAS, NEVADA

(3)

will be you. Wow I bet you'll be just like an angel.
Well Mrs. M, soon to be. I'll be calling you
in a few hrs to talk to you & to tell you I love you over
& over again. So until then darling

All My Love
Always + Forever
(Your Guy) Rudi

My Dearest Plus;

Darling it was real wonderful talking to you earlier this evening. I'm glad you were feeling a lot better. Everytime you feel good, I feel good also and when you feel sad, I'm sad too. I know its hard being away from each other, but the only way to overcome that is to always think of the future + when we'll be together always. I love you so very very much.

The show is going great here so far + every nite we've had to turn people away. I hope it stays like this for the rest of the engagement.

I'm real glad that the plans for the wedding are going real wonderful. Honest I wish I was there to help you with them

It would really be wonderful. But whatever you do darling don't let anything upset or make you sick, because I just know everything going to turn out real wonderful. I can hardly wait till June 11th comes. It'll be a day we'll never forget.

I guess that's the latest news for you darling. I'll write you again to-morrow, and I'll be phoning you on Tuesday.

All My Love,
Always + Forever
(Your Guy) Rudi

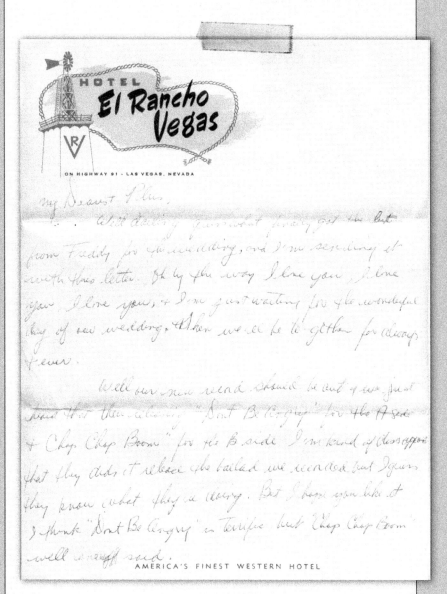

HOTEL
El Rancho Vegas
ON HIGHWAY 91 · LAS VEGAS, NEVADA

My Dearest Plus,

Well darling you won't finally get the best
from Freddy for the wedding, and I'm sending it
with this letter. Oh by the way I love you, I love
you, I love you, + I'm just waiting for the wonderful
day of our wedding. Then we'll be together for always
& ever.

Well our new record should be out & we just
heard that their releasing "Don't Be Angry" for the A side
& "Chop Chop Boom" for the B side I'm kind of disappointed
that they didn't release the ballad we recorded but I guess
they know what they're doing. But I hope you like it.
I think "Don't Be Angry" is terrific but "Chop Chop Boom"
well enough said.

AMERICA'S FINEST WESTERN HOTEL

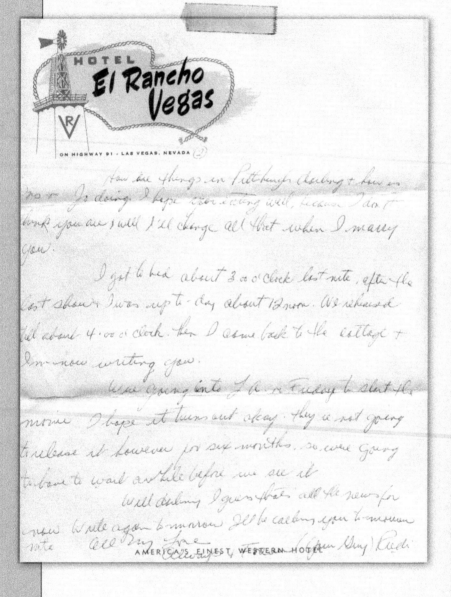

HOTEL
El Rancho Vegas
ON HIGHWAY 91 · LAS VEGAS, NEVADA

How are things in Pittsburgh darling + how is
ma + Jo doing I hope your doing well, because I don't
think you are & well I'll change all that when I marry
you.

I got to bed about 3.00 o'clock last nite, after the
last show & I was up to-day about 12 noon. We rehearsed
till about 4.00 o'clock. then I came back to the cottage +
I'm now writing you.

We're going into LA on Friday to start the
movie I hope it turns out okay. they're not going
to release it however for six months. so we're going
to have to wait awhile before we see it.

Well darling I guess that's all the news for
now. Write again tomorrow I'll be calling you tomorrow
nite. All My Love
Always (Your Guy) Riedi

AMERICA'S FINEST WESTERN HOTEL

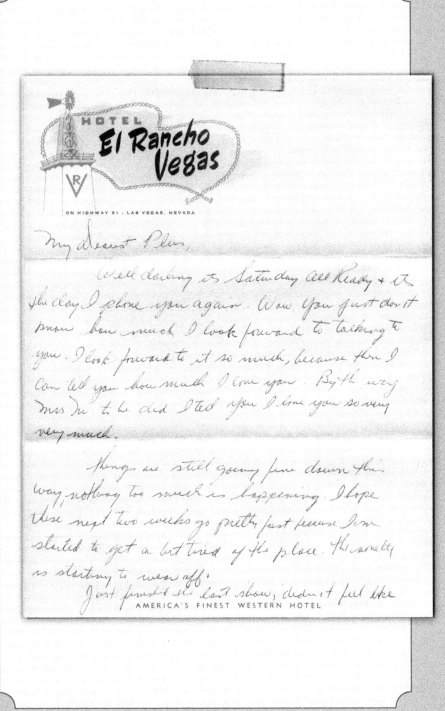

HOTEL El Rancho Vegas

ON HIGHWAY 91 · LAS VEGAS, NEVADA

My dearest Plus,

Well darling its Saturday all Ready & its the day I phone you again. Wow you just don't know how much I look forward to talking to you. I look forward to it so much, because then I can tell you how much I love you. By the way miss In to be did I tell you I love you so very very much.

Things are still going fine down this way, nothing too much is happening. I hope these next two weeks go pretty fast because I've started to get a bit tired of the place. The novelty is starting to wear off.

Just finish the last show, didn't feel like

AMERICA'S FINEST WESTERN HOTEL

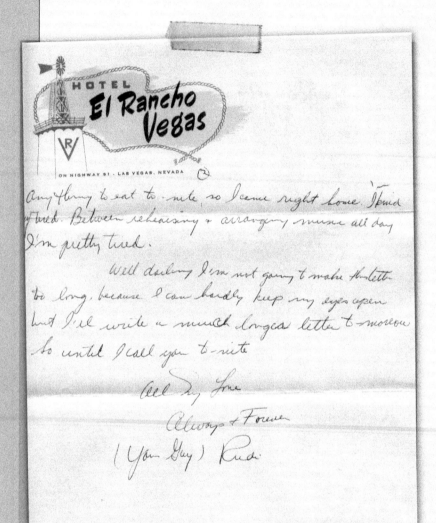

HOTEL
El Rancho Vegas

ON HIGHWAY 91 · LAS VEGAS, NEVADA

Any thing to eat to-nite, so I came right home. I'm kind of tired. Between rehearsing & arranging music all day I'm pretty tired.

Well darling I'm not going to make this letter too long, because I can hardly keep my eyes open but I'll write a much longer letter to-morrow so until I call you to-nite

All my Love
Always & Forever
(Your Guy) Rudi

AMERICA'S FINEST WESTERN HOTEL

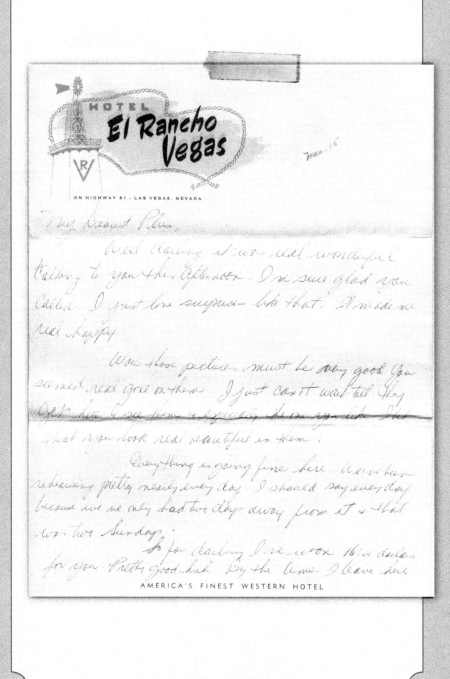

HOTEL
El Rancho Vegas

ON HIGHWAY 91 · LAS VEGAS, NEVADA

Mar. 16

My Dearest Plus,

Well darling it was real wonderful talking to you this afternoon. I'm sure glad you called. I just love surprises like that. It made me real happy.

Wow those pictures must be very good you seemed real gone on them. I just can't wait till they get here & see them & especially the one you like & that you look real beautiful in them.

Everything is going fine here. We have been rehearsing pretty nearly every day. I should say every day because we we only had two days away from it & that was two Sundays.

So far darling I've won 16:00 dollars for you. Pretty good luck. By the time I leave here

AMERICA'S FINEST WESTERN HOTEL

HOTEL El Rancho Vegas

ON HIGHWAY 91 · LAS VEGAS, NEVADA

I should have some more to add to that Wow!

I've been going to bed about 2:30 every nite & getting up about 11 o'clock. Haven't to much time to get a tan, but I'm trying honey. I'd like to have one by the time I get to Chicago, then I won't have to put any make up on anymore.

Well darling I'll be writing again tomorrow & I'll be calling you also; & darling you don't know what a wonderful feeling it gives me, to talk to you like I did this afternoon & find that you're so happy. It gives me a real warm feeling inside. I love you, I love you, I love you.

All My Love
Always & Forever
(Your Guy) Rudi.

AMERICA'S FINEST WESTERN HOTEL

My dearest Plum,

Well darling another letter to-day. Wow this is terrific. I hope your getting one from me every day because I'm mailing one every day. If we keep this up, how could we ever get sad.

Darling things are going real wonderful here, but as I told you they've just changed our bookings around, we'll only be here another three weeks, then we go to Reno for a week, then to the Chicago theatre for three weeks. I can hardly wait to get back East again. And darling don't forget to try & arrange for a couple of days to come to Chicago. I am sweating from day to day till I see you there. Oh its time to tell you I love you, I love you I love you

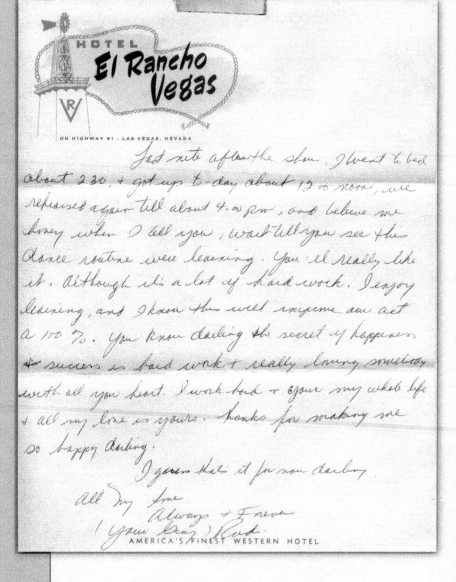

HOTEL
El Rancho Vegas

ON HIGHWAY 91 · LAS VEGAS, NEVADA

Last nite after the show, I went to bed about 2:30, & got up to-day about 12:00 noon, we rehearsed again till about 4.00 p.m., and believe me honey when I tell you, wait till you see the dance routine were learning. You'll really like it. Although it's a lot of hard work. I enjoy learning, and I know this will improve our act a 100 %. You know darling the secret of happiness & success is hard work & really loving somebody with all your heart. I work hard & your my whole life & all my love is yours. thanks for making me so happy darling.

I guess that's it for now darling.

All my love
Always & Forever
(your Gary) Rick.

AMERICA'S FINEST WESTERN HOTEL

My Dear+ Plus,

Well darling we just finished the last show & I'm now getting ready for bed & believe me when I say boy am I tired. We had a real rough day t-day.

We had a four hr recording session in L.A. and it sure knocked us out. We were up at 7.oo o'clock this morning, caught a 9.oo o'clock plane for L.A. arrived there about 10.30 & started our recording session at 12.oo It lasted til 4.oo o'clock. Then we caught a 5o'clock plane back & arrived here at 6.45, and then got ready for the show.

The session went off well, and we don't know what their going to release next out of the sides we cut, but whatever it is it should be out by

AMERICA'S FINEST WESTERN HOTEL

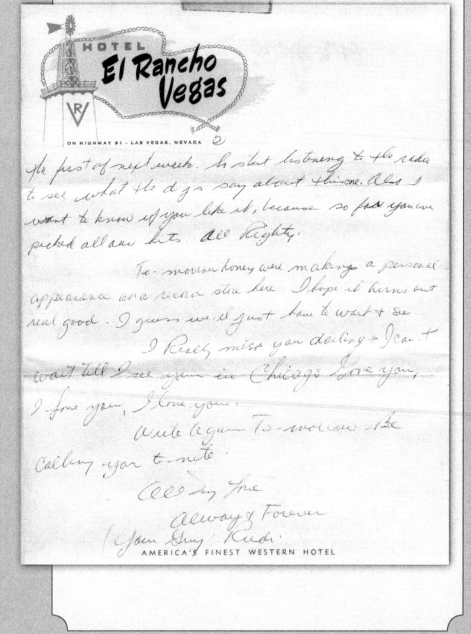

HOTEL
El Rancho Vegas

ON HIGHWAY 91 · LAS VEGAS, NEVADA

the first of next week. So start listening to the radio to see what the d.j.s say about this one. Also I want to know if you like it, because so far you've picked all our hits. All Righty.

To-morrow honey we're making a personal appearance at a record store here. I hope it turns out real good. I guess we'll just have to wait & see.

I Really miss you darling & I can't wait till I see you in Chicago. I love you, I love you, I love you.

Write again To-morrow. Be calling you to-nite.

All my love
Always & Forever
Your Guy Rudi

AMERICA'S FINEST WESTERN HOTEL

HOTEL
El Rancho Vegas

ON HIGHWAY 91 · LAS VEGAS, NEVADA

My Dearest Plas;

Well darling we just arrived
from L.A. We left early this morning. Did
the movie + left their at 5.00 this evening arrived
back here, about 7.00 pm — now I've got a
lot of time to write you.

Everything went real great to-day
+ I think it will be a very good movie short. They'll
probably release it in about 3 or 4 months.

Darling I'm real worried about you
fainting the other day, please take real good
care of yourself huh. I don't want anything to
happen to you — especially now.

Wow I can hardly wait till we
get married. I'm really getting that

AMERICA'S FINEST WESTERN HOTEL

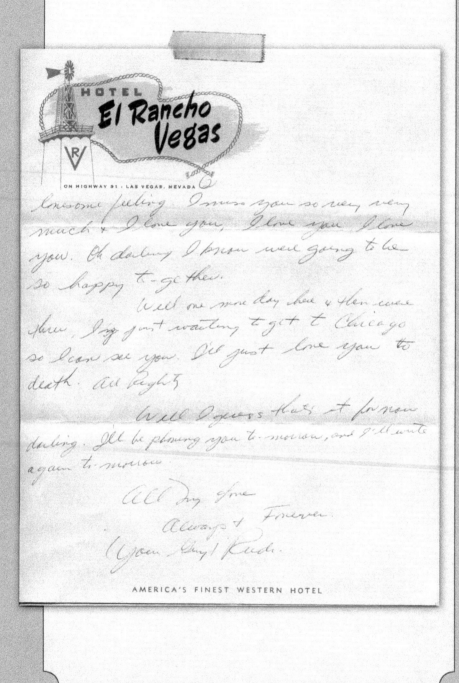

HOTEL
**El Rancho
Vegas**

ON HIGHWAY 91 · LAS VEGAS, NEVADA

lonesome feeling. I miss you so very very
much & I love you, I love you I love
you. Oh darling I know we're going to be
so happy to-gether.

Well one more day here & then come
there, I'm just waiting to get to Chicago
so I can see you. I'll just love you to
death. All right?

Well I guess that's it for now
darling. I'll be phoning you to-morrow, and I'll write
again to-morrow.

All my love
Always & Forever.
Your Guy / Rudi.

AMERICA'S FINEST WESTERN HOTEL

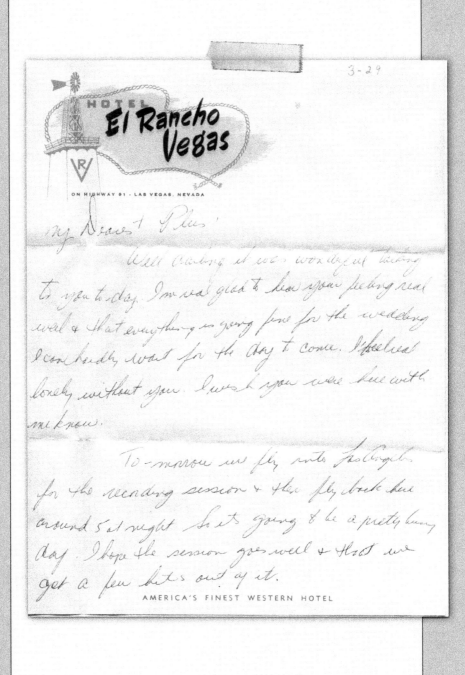

HOTEL
El Rancho Vegas

ON HIGHWAY 91 · LAS VEGAS, NEVADA

My Dearest Plus,

Well darling it was wonderful talking
to you today. I'm real glad to hear your feeling real
well & that everything is going fine for the wedding.
I can hardly wait for the day to come. I feel real
lonely without you. I wish you were here with
me now.

To-morrow we fly into Los Angeles
for the recording session & then fly back here
around 5 at night so it's going to be a pretty busy
day. I hope the session goes well & that we
get a few hits out of it.

AMERICA'S FINEST WESTERN HOTEL

We've been pretty busy this la' week
rehearsing every day with Dave for about 3 or 4 hrs
a day. It's been a real grind.

Darling I've been getting a lot of
rest + I feel pretty good. So by the time I see you in
Chicago I should be feeling real great! All Righty

Well darling I'm not going to make
this letter too long I'll write again to-morrow. I have
to get ready for the show now. I'll call you on Sat.

All my love

Always + Forever
(Your Guy) Rudi

HOTEL **Riverside** RENO, NEVADA

My Dearest Plus,

Well darling we are now in Reno.
We arrived here about 10:30 this morning, its
about noon now & I have to rehearse the band
in about 2 hrs.

We finished in Vegas (as you know) Tuesday
nite, caught an early flight at 8:00 o'clock into
San Francisco arrived there about 9:00 pm. We spent
the day there seeing all the disc jockeys up until
about 3:00 o'clock in the morning. Got a bit of sleep & we
were up about 6:00 o'clock this morning to catch the
plane here into Reno. So I'm pretty tired.

I can hardly wait till I get
to Chicago to see you. I'm glad we're only here
for a week, I'll be real happy to get back east again
because that means I'll be seeing you in about
2 weeks & the sooner the better. I miss you so
very very much & I'm real real lonesome. I love

you. I love you, I love you.

I hope that your feeling well darling, it seems to me that your not getting enough rest or eating well. Please try to take real good care of yourself because I worry so much.

I'll be phoning you in about 4 hrs + I promise I'll phone on time this time. I was real hurt about the last time, and it'll never happen again.

I guess that all for now darling I'll write again tonite.

All my love
Always+Forever

(Your Guy) Rich

HOTEL **Riverside** RENO, NEVADA

My Dearest Plus;

Well darling here we are loving each other + missing each other so much that we're starting to quarrel over things that really don't matter at all.

After hanging up the other nite, I was very hurt but thought it was so foolish for us to quarrel because actually the only reason it happens is because we're so lonely + our nerves get a bit keyed up + we're apt to jump at things that don't mean anything at all.

I like to say with all the love that's in my heart for you darling. if I said anything to hurt you that nite. I'm so very very sorry. may I be thoughtful enough to never ever let it happen again. I miss you I love you + always will. Please always remember this.

Things have been going swell down here, but I'll be sure glad when I get to Chicago. Darling I can hardly wait till I see you. I love you, I love you I love you.

②

We've been kept pretty busy, we're still rehearsing quite a bit & I've been getting enough rest to keep me going for years. I've been going right to bed after the last show & I feel real great.

Oh By the way - the juke box operators had a big convention in Chicago (from all over the USA) & guess what, they picked our new record "Don't Be Angry" as the "Best of the year" which is quite an honor.

I guess that's all the news for now darling, I'll be calling you to-nite - I'll write again to-morrow.

All My Love - Always + Forever
Your Guy
Rick.

HOTEL **Riverside** RENO, NEVADA

My Dearest Plas;

Well darling its Sunday, already
only a few more days here, then to Chicago
where I'll be seeing you. I hope the time goes
real fast. I can hardly wait till I see you.
I miss you so very very much. Darling in
a short while we'll be together for always
+ ever. I'm never going to let you out of my
sight for one minute. I love you, I love you
I love you

Last nite we had the show, so
we didn't get thru till about 3.30 + I went
right to bed. This afternoon I had to rehearse
the band again, we have what we call a relief
band just for tonite, so I had to rehearse them
again. So I feel a little tired now.

You sounded real tired over the phone
last nite. I hope your not working too hard
+ taking real good care of yourself. I don't

(2)

were anything to happen to you. All Rights.

Things have been going real great last
nite I was talking to the boss + he really likes us. He
wants us to come back in October that'd be great
huh, and the crowd last nite was terrific. It's
the best Saturday nite they've had here since the
summer which is their best season here.

From all reports our new record
is starting to move pretty good. As for Pittsburgh
we don't even worry about it. It seems like nothing
ever happens there anymore.

I guess that's all the news now
darling I'll write again to-morrow.

All My Love
Always + Forever
(Your Guy) Rudi

Chapter Eight

THE CALL

CHAPTER 8: THE CALL

April 1955: Good Friday

I worked the night shift, and then took a cab to the Pittsburgh bus station and the bus to Uniontown. Heading home for the holiday, I thought about last Good Friday, and then Saturday; buying the record, plotting to see the Crew-Cuts at the Copa. What a great year it had been. We'd come full circle! I'd handed in my resignation, my contract would be fulfilled and in a month I'd be moving home. There were so many things to complete before the wedding, preparing for all the out-of-town guests. Everything had been going so well.

The Crew-Cuts would be appearing at the Copa the week before the wedding. They were looking forward to some time off, while I'd be honeymooning with my Crew-Cut. After our honeymoon in New York, we would continue together on to London where the group would be appearing for the Empire Theater Group for two or three months in England and Scotland. I looked forward to traveling with them. We all got along so well and I really cared about them.

I had a cup of coffee with my mom upon arrival, then off to bed. I asked her to wake me for dinner, and told her that Rudi would be calling in the evening.

She woke me around five o'clock saying, "Rudi is on the phone." Half-asleep, I didn't realize that the call was a couple of hours early.

"Hi, honey," I said.

"I'm sorry to wake you," he said.

"You don't have to be sorry, ever. In two months, I'll be right beside you when you wake me. I can't wait!"

Silence... no sweet comment. He sounded strange. "We have to postpone the wedding."

I thought I was dreaming. "I'm sorry – what are you saying?"

"We have to postpone the wedding."

"Why?" Then I became frightened. "Are you ill?"

"No."

"One of the guys?"

"No..."

"Your folks?"

"No!"

"Rudi, on the desk in my room there are 220 invitations addressed and stamped, ready to mail. Eight hundred cocktail napkins saying 'June 11, 1955 Rudi and Placeda,' 400 matchboxes printed with 'Rudi and Plus.' I can see my gown hanging on the closet door. Please talk to me, the girl you love more than life, the one you would never hurt!"

Again, silence.

"I deserve an explanation. If you can't give me one, there won't be a postponement, it will be canceled."

"No," he said.

"Oh my God, Rudi you broke your commitment, you cheated on me, you did! Please say something..." My voice is starting to crack. "Oh, Rudi, not you! I have trusted you so."

I felt like I was spinning into darkness. I didn't recognize my own voice.

"Please call me when you can talk to me and tell me what is happening. Good bye."

He never called.

As I hung up and went running to my room, I passed the kitchen where Mom and Charlie were making dinner. "What is it, Placeda?"

Mom called out. I was crying really hard now, but I managed to replay our conversation. She was in shock; this couldn't be. Was this what they call pre-wedding jitters, or cold feet?

"It will pass," said Mother, "I've never known of any man to love a woman as much as Rudi loves you. He will call back." Immediately I called my three best friends and swore them to secrecy. They could not believe what I was saying, and they agreed with Mom.

Two reasons to keep this quiet; all agreed this will pass, and secondly we were all set to go to my favorite cousin Dee and Bob's wedding later this month in Ohio. I definitely didn't want to interrupt the excitement and joy of her big wedding. She was expecting 300 guests. Besides, by then, Rudi would be back.

Mo, Jo, and I got back to the apartment Easter evening.

We sat down on the bed. "Here, here…" I said, as I dropped all the Vegas letters on the bed, "We are going to read each one of these. I must see if I missed something in these letters, a clue to what may have happened. Did I ignore something?"

I'd never shared my letters from Rudi with my friends before, although sometimes I would read them a little bit; where the Crew-Cuts were appearing, how the show was going, the records, something Rudi would want me to tell them. But now I needed their help, to try to figure out this phone call saying he wanted to postpone the wedding. I was still in shock. In his last letter, dated April 4th, he was so loving, so happy about our plans, so anxious to get to Chicago where I would be waiting.

The phone call I'd gotten from him on April 6th had given no indication of anything but him being happy and moving forward with our plans.

Was I right to assume that he'd cheated? That was bad – but under certain circumstances, we decided, there might have been a reasonable excuse, and maybe it was fixable. But he hadn't offered a reason! I was hurt and upset, so I gave him time to rethink what he had said.

There had been a letter on March 3rd in which he'd apologized for going out with the guys. We'd discussed this on the phone; he was so sorry, he didn't want me going out, and so he promised not to do it again. We went on to make plans for his return to Chicago where we could be together. He had asked me so many times on the phone to come to Vegas, even for a weekend.

I'd never thought it was serious — if I had, I would have flown out in a second. I was working extra shifts, and I thought it was just him missing me, since this was the longest we had been apart since becoming engaged. It is amazing how you think you know everything at 22, but I was just naive. I would have bet my life that this moral man would never, ever let me down. Never!

Combing through the letters now, we saw that he was extremely busy; taking dancing lessons, changing the group's routines, flying back and forth to Hollywood to make the movie and recording. Just a really tough schedule, I'd thought.

I gave it a week before I tried to contact him, but I could not get through. I tried their manager, Fred S., who gave me no information. After another week, I called Fred again. This time, he said to send him the bills for the deposits and any wedding-related expenses we had incurred.

Mo, Jo, and I flew to Chicago three days before Dee's wedding. We left Chicago in thirty-six hours, not having been able to see either Rudi or Fred. We flew to Ohio for the wedding.

Dee and Bob's Wedding

Dee and Bob's wedding was beautiful, but so painful for me. Well-meaning family and friends kept coming up to me, wishing me happiness, saying how much they liked Rudi, and what a great addition to the family he was – and I couldn't say a thing.

As the evening wore on and the people had a few drinks, I was Mrs. Crew-Cut, their celebrity. I would be a beautiful bride like my cousin. By 11:30 that night, when it came time for the bridal dance (an ethnic custom), I couldn't hold back the tears as I was kissing my cousin goodbye. Everyone thought they were tears of joy and excitement. Only five people there and I knew how my heart was breaking. Unfortunately, this was just the beginning.

We flew back to Pittsburgh the next day; we said for work, but in truth it was to start making moving arrangements. We girls always tried to work the same shift, but I asked to work nights the last week. I wouldn't have to deal with so many people, and it was cruelly hard to be always happy and smiling.

Mo and Jo were working days, usually getting home about 4:30. I would get up then, and sometimes take a nap before leaving for work about 10:15 P.M. I was having a hard time sleeping these last three weeks. There'd been so much to deal with. One afternoon, I was awakened by the sound of the apartment door opening. I looked at the clock on the night table, and it was only 2:30 in the afternoon. I heard whispering, and asked out loud, "Who is it?"

Mo and Jo answered together, "It's us, don't get up, stay in bed."

The phone rang, and Mo answered quickly; a few whispers, and she hung up. They were standing in the doorway of the bedroom. I sat up in bed, turned on the light, and looked at their faces. "I know something has happened, what is it? Is it my mother or Rudi?"

They looked at each other, and Mo angrily said, "He's married! The bastard got married just before we got to Chicago."

I sat there for minutes that somehow felt like an hour. Then I started to cry, and so did they. I cried so hard I got the hiccups, and then could hardly breathe. We knew I couldn't work that night. I knew I was in shock.

We sat up most of the night. It was like a wake.

May 7, 1955: Saturday Evening

Mo, Jo, and I arrived home that Friday morning and worked all day, unpacking and repacking two big suitcases each. We were leaving for Miami Beach, Florida on Sunday, Mother's Day.

Notes had been written and were being sent out today. Some family and close friends, who were expecting a beautiful invitation this week, would be receiving a cancellation note. Others would be notified by phone. I thought that notes would be easier, so I had been writing them for the last two weeks. I don't even know how many had teardrops on them.

The boxes of wedding invitations, the eight hundred cocktail napkins saying June 11, 1955 Rudi & Placeda, and the four hundred matchboxes printed with the date and Rudi & Plus, were discretely tucked in the back of the guest closet.

On Saturday morning, I talked to my stepfather. I told him what I wanted to do with them, and he was in. Now we went to Mom, who I think still wanted to keep them 'till June 11th.

That evening, Charlie and I drove out to his brother's home in the country. He had put a large, empty, metal tub in the backyard. We dumped the invitations and napkins in, but stopped when it came to the matches. The men promised that they would take care of them. I had 143 love letters plus cards in boxes, but could not bring myself to give them up. They went back to the closet in my room. The next time I came home, six months later, they were gone. I never asked where.

The cigarette case/lighter that Rudi had given me for graduation was a beautiful dark purple enamel with my initials, P.D., mono-grammed in gold, with room for the M. to be added on. The inscription inside read:

Congratulations Darling
All My Love
Always and Forever
Your Guy Rudi

I clicked the lighter, lit one of the invitations and dropped it in the tub, where it quickly ignited. Then, I dropped the cigarette case in, too. Both men jumped, thinking I had accidentally dropped it, but when they looked at my face in the light of the fire, they knew better.

Charlie and I thanked his brother, then we drove home. I was quiet, and he asked me if having our little bonfire had made me feel better, I lied and said, "Yes." They wanted so much to see me smile again, and I really tried. Did I want to talk?

"No."

"That's okay, honey."

As we walked in, Mom called, "Placeda, I just made a pot of tea, come join me and have some pound cake." She made the best pound cake. We were coffee drinkers, and the only time we had tea was if someone was sick or there was a serious conversation to be had. The tea always seemed very comforting.

Charlie took his dessert in the living room to watch T.V. Mom and I sat in the kitchen. I was leaving early in the morning, and she was worried about me, I hadn't been eating or sleeping very much. This was our last chance to talk. I was concerned about leaving them to deal with canceling the arrangements. The newspaper here would probably call, maybe even the Pittsburgh paper. I asked her please to only speak with the hometown papers, since they had always been very kind to me. She assured me she and Charlie would tie up all the loose ends. She said, "Please don't worry, honey, we are pleased to help in any way we can."

I said, "Mom, he is dead."

She was cutting the cake and looked up, very startled. "Who is dead?"

"Rudi," I said.

"Did you have a bad dream?"

"No."

"A premonition?"

I shook my head no, tears rolling down my cheeks. I replied, "This is how I will have to think of what has happened, so I can get on with my life." Pre-divorce or breakup there are arguments, anger, unkind words, doubt, bitterness. But, in March, I'd received loving phone calls and more than twenty love letters, until two days before that devastating phone call.

In this last month, I'd gone through shock, disbelief, rejection and, soon, humiliation and tears – oh, so many tears – now some anger, but I didn't even have the energy to be angry. Now, I just wanted to finish grieving and hopefully move on.

Jo's sister, Marie, would be going with us. Her parents would be driving us to Pittsburgh Airport. The news of the broken engagement and Rudi's marriage would be breaking Monday morning.

Leaving Allegheny General Hospital

When we'd realized a couple weeks ago I would be leaving, I felt I had to get out of Pennsylvania. Mo and Jo handed in their resignations, and we decided it would be Florida for all of us. May 6th we would be leaving A.G.H. and Pittsburgh. So much had happened in three and a half years, especially this last year. Now, at 22 years old, it seemed all the magic had suddenly disappeared.

We settled into our seats on the plane, Jo next to me. I told her I didn't want anything to eat or drink, just wanted to sleep and figure out how my near-perfect life had come to an end so abruptly. I still had no answers.

I sat in my seat at the window, pretending to sleep. I counted the many beautiful shades of blue in the sky, watched as the puffy white clouds floated by the window, blocking the view for an instant, then moving on. Soon I was looking down on them, no longer eye level.

I wondered how I could be so sad, looking at something so beautiful.

These girls were like my guardian angels, protecting me even from Crew-Cut songs. If they came on the radio, they rushed to turn them off. I told a few friends that I never wanted to see his face, or hear his voice, again. I'm sure he got this message.

My mom was awakened that Monday morning by a reporter knocking on her door. She was inundated with phone calls from magazines and newspapers, from Uniontown, Pittsburgh, New York, Cleveland, Lorain, Chicago, Los Angeles, Vegas, Reno, Canada, and others.

Lawyers called, wanting to represent me in a suit against Rudi for alienation of affection. I had never heard of this before, but apparently it was legitimate grounds for a lawsuit. I obviously would never sue.

Chapter Nine

THE FALL OUT

CHAPTER 9: THE FALL OUT

May 1955: Florida, and the New Hospital

We vacationed at a small hotel in Miami Beach on Collins Avenue. Jo and her family had been there before, and they felt it was a safe spot for us. The weather was great and we all got terrible sunburns, even me, who never burned. That gave me an excuse to stay in one night, alone. Once we got off the plane in Miami, I told myself, "No more tears," at least not for the girls to see. They were here to enjoy a much-needed vacation, sun, fun, and, maybe for them, dates.

This night I had room service, and I sat alone thinking about the last time I was in a hotel room. It was February in St. Louis, getting ready for the show, feeling happy, and trying to look pretty for someone who loved me. Of course the tears started. It seemed as if that night was so long ago.

Tomorrow, we were going for our interviews. It was a small private hospital in Coral Gables. We had sent applications and letters to the Nursing Administrator.

We did have a wonderful doctor friend who knew Mrs. C. He gave her his word we were not merely Allegheny General Graduates, but were the best trained, most professional, compassionate young ladies, and she would be so lucky to have us.

If our interviews went well, we would look for a house or an apartment close to the hospital. We would be returning our rental car in a week.

The fourth roommate, Marie, was a secretary, and she said she wouldn't mind if she had to take a bus, since we three would be leaving earlier in the mornings and maybe working different shifts.

Our interviews were more or less a formality. We were hired that very day. Jo would be the head nurse on Labor and Maternity, Mo on Medical, and me, on Surgical. We would be starting in ten days.

Our first day we woke at 5:30 A.M. to a very sunny, hot and humid morning. We hadn't had our uniforms on for three weeks. They were long sleeved, heavily starched, and not too comfortable. We walked to the hospital in seventeen minutes, and were there at 6:20 for breakfast. At 6:45, we were on our respective floors, being introduced to the night nurses and day crew.

We had to be oriented to our new surroundings by the night supervisor and Mrs. C. I can say the first week was tough. We were not welcomed with open arms by all. They were wondering where we'd come from, and how we'd landed these head positions.

In fact, the first three or four weeks, we came in early and stayed late, because we took our new positions very seriously. Every hospital does things somewhat differently. It was harder to adjust than we'd thought.

When we got home, we were so tired and hot, totally exhausted most evenings. I barely had the energy to shower, and sometimes dinner would only be toast. We would actually fall in bed into a really deep sleep. We were not yet acclimated to the hot, humid climate.

The only good part of this was that I was just too tired to think too much about Rudi.

Local Girl Is Cold To Dan Cupid

Wed-May 11-1955

MISS CONTEEN

Preferring nursing to a marital career, Uniontown's former Beauty Queen has called off her previously proposed marriage to a famous vocal artist and is now vacationing in Florida.

Formerly engaged to Rudi Maugeri, a member of the nationally-famed Canadian quartet popularly known as the Crew-Cuts, Placeda Dee Conteen, "Miss Uniontown" of 1951, is sojourning in Miami and according to her mother, Mrs. Charles Dzamba, 120 E. Main St., may favor transferring her professional career to the Southland.

Since her graduation from Allegheny General Hospital School of Nursing in 1954, Miss Conteen has been a member of the nursing staff of that Pittsburgh hospital. She is also a graduate of North Union Twp. High School, Class of 1951.

A native of Toronto, Canada, her former fiance, since the breakup of his betrothal to the Uniontown nurse, is reported to have been married in Chicago to Cynthia Brooks of Dallas, Tex. The Crew-Cuts, recording artists, have a singing engagement in Pittsburgh May 30.

Front page of the home town paper, The Morning Herald.

Pittsburgh Sun-Telegraph

Vol. 56—No. 99   In Three Sections—Section One   WEDNESDAY, MAY 11, 1955   *****   FIVE CENTS

JILTED . . . Placeda Conteen, Uniontown beauty queen who was jilted by a member of the Crew Cuts, was mighty happy when this picture was taken in December, 1954. Her engagement had just been announced, and she pointed to her fiance's picture.

Sun-Telegraph Photo by Edwin J. Morgan

"Jilted" says it all.

Singer Jilts Uniontown Girl

Placeda Conteen, the Uniontown beauty queen and a former nurse at Allegheny General Hospital, p r o b a b l y was humming a new tune today, the one called "Jilted."

On June 11, she was to have married Rudi Maugeri, a member of the Crew Cuts' vocal quartet, but two weeks ago he married a dancer from Dallas, Miss Connie Brooks.

The pert and pretty Placeda, "Miss Uniontown of 1951," was vacationing in Miami today, t r y i n g to forget the whole thing, according to her mother, Mrs. Vera Dzamba, of Uniontown.

Maugeri and the 22-year-old Placeda met at the Copa in May, 1954, and announced their engagement there last December.

'I Can't Wed You, My Wife Won't Let Me'

PLACEDA CONTEEN
Fiance married another.

* * *

That, in Nutshell, Explains Breakup Of Beauty, Singer

If there is a theme song to explain the break-up of the engagement of Beauty Queen Placeda Conteen, of Uniontown, and Rudi Maugeri, a member of the Crew Cuts, a singing group, it is a snatch from the old English Music Hall ballad:

"I can't get away to marry you today, my wife won't let me."

Former Nurse in City

That was the situation disclosed last night by Mrs. Vera Dzamba, of Uniontown, mother of 22-year-old Placeda, who won the Miss Uniontown title in 1951 at the age of 17.

Miss Conteen, formerly a nurse at Allegheny General Hospital and winner of third place in the 1951 Miss Pennsylvania contest, announced her engagement to Maugeri in December last year.

Maugeri, a Canadian, married another girl about two weeks ago, Mrs. Dzamba said last night.

"We heard about it," Mrs. Dzamba said. "So I called up to confirm it. Maugeri said he married somebody else. To make sure I called Fred Strauss, the manager of the Crew Cuts, whose office is in Cleveland. He confirmed Maugeri's marriage to another girl."

Mother Also Won Contest

"There wasn't anything else to do except call off the marriage."

Mrs. Dzamba said her daughter is in Florida in seclusion to avoid publicity over the breakup of the en-

(Continued on Page 4, Col. 1)

Can Not Wed, He Has Wife

(Continued from Page 1)

gagement to the Canadian vocalist.

Miss Conteen comes by her beauty winning ways by inheritance. Mrs. Dzamba, the former Vera McCall, won a Uniontown beauty crown in 1928.

Fuller Explanation Hinted

A fuller explanation of what happened might be forthcoming on May 30 when the Crew Cuts begin a week's engagement at the Copa. It was at the Copa that Placeda and Rudi met in May, 1954 and it was there that the engagement was announced in December last year.

The week of June 6 had been set aside by the Music Corporation of America, the Crew Cuts agents, as a week when Rudi would be unavailable because of his honeymoon with Placeda, according to Lenny Litman, Copa manager.

DOROTHY KILGALLEN:

Marilyn to Be 3 Stories Tall

NEW YORK—There'll be a three-story-high replica of Marilyn Monroe outside Loew's State when "Seven Year Itch" opens next month. Plus a gimmick: a wind machine will blow up her pleated skirt—as in the famous news picture—24 hours a day.

Greta Garbo has found herself a perfect hideout—in Montauk Point. The locals know her as "Miss Grace."

This big show biz announcement may be upcoming soon: Mike Todd to put "South Pacific" into film production with Gene Nelson as Lt. Cable and Judy Garland as Nellie Forbush.

Barbara Hutton, who can't resist buying baubles for the fellows she loves, has ordered star sapphire studs for millionaire Hal Hayes . . . J. P. Marquard's best-selling novel, "Sincerely, Willis Wayde," has been shelved as a TV drama idea. The brass felt it might offend big business.

THE CREW cuts no longer are all bachelors. Rudi Maugeri just confided the secret: He's been married 10 days to ~~Gloria Brown~~, a dancer he met when the singing quartet played Las Vegas. Rudi's fans will be as flabbergasted by the news as his partners were: He was scheduled to waltz down the aisle on June 11th with a Pittsburgh nurse, Placida Dee Contine.

Paul Gregory has asked Greer Garson to consider the leading feminine role in the version of Dickens' "Bleak House" that John Patrick is preparing.

Joan Bennett's daughter, Melinda Markey, will be in New York later this month, hoping to land a few roles in summer stock.

Alfred Lunt is well on the road to recovery after the operation . . . The Patti Page-Charles O'Curran romance seems to be losing impetus . . . Church and charity groups have found a way to get around their troubles with bingo games and the cops—a loophole based on a court ruling of some years ago. It involves games of chance "offered as incidental part of an entertainment for which a charge is levied" . . . Terry Moore's got herself a bullfighter, just like the other girls. He's Juan Posado, out of Madrid.

HOLLYWOOD'S latest Topic A revolves around a screen beauty who is married to one of the handsomest men in the world. But she's fallen for a not-at-all handsome (though successful) writer-producer, who must have great magic because so many of Movieland's most glamorous women have cared for him deeply. Whenever they are together in public, off the set, they are discreetly chaperoned by another member of the cast of the picture she's starring in. But that doesn't fool the Hollywood citizens who know what a blockbuster he is. It is written in her eyes.

Very famous gossip columnist, at the time.

She Was Like a Sister, He Married Other Girl

And, That's the Story of a Broken Engagement of Crew Cut and Beauty Queen

BY VINCE JOHNSON
Post-Gazette Staff Writer

Rudi Maugeri, a member of the Crew Cuts, had two songs to sing for two different girls when the quartet opened an engagement last night at the Copa.

"Don't Be Angry" was for Placeda Conteen, the Uniontown beauty queen Rudi once intended to marry—but didn't.

"Earth Angel" was for ~~Constance Brooks, the Dallas dancer~~ he hadn't intended to marry—but did.

What happened to break up his engagement with Miss Conteen and to produce his marriage to ~~Miss Brooks~~ is a long story. It takes more than one man to tell it. So bend one ear to Rudi and another to his manager, Fred Strauss.

"He didn't jilt Miss Conteen. Their engagement was broken in February. He didn't meet ~~Miss Brooks~~ until March," said Mr. Strauss.

"Placeda and I had an disagreement. She's not in show business and it's hard for her to understand," chimed in Rudi.

"Rudy's phone bills when he was calling Placeda long-distance were fantastic. About $200 a month," winced Mr. Strauss. *who said*

"I had given her an engagement ring and we had put away a wedding ring," recalled Rudi.

"She was like a sister to the Crew Cuts," said Mr. Strauss, looking very brotherly.

"A week before ~~Constance~~ and I were married, Placeda came to Chicago to see if we could be reconciled. But it was all off," said Rudi.

Rudi was asked the whereabouts of his bride. "In Dallas, visiting her folks. She'll be here Tuesday," he said.

"It's miserable for a girl to go through this," mentioned Mr. Strauss, meaning the traveling incident to show business."

"Yeah," said Rudi.

"But they're getting along fine, of course," reassured Mr. Strauss.

"No scraps at all. Later, we're going to raise a family," declared Rudi.

Rudi thumbed through a sheaf of fan mail and produced a letter from a Chinese girl, Leticia Yap, living in Manila in the Philippines.

"Before Rudi was married, girls worshiped him as an artist. It was teen-age idolization. Now they want to be motherly toward him and protective," said Mr. Strauss.

There was no break up in Feb. as anyone can see from the Feb & March's letter sent & never contacted the press

Pittsburgh Sun-Telegraph

DEAR BUDDY:
Here's News From Home

By KENNETH SPEER

BUDDIES, the "Fountain of Youth" in North Park had to be closed—the water is contaminated . . . Gov. Leader suspended boxing in Pennsylvania for 90 days while investigation is made of charges that a fighter was doped in Philadelphia . . . Rudi Maugeri, of the Crew Cuts quartet, jilted Placeda Conteen, lovely Uniontown nurse, and married a Dallas dancer.

DEBBIE REYNOLDS

Debbie Reynolds is going over to see you buddies in Korea . . . FBI arrested James Cox, 25, and Theodore Perkins, 26, in Hill District apartment here after $20,000 payroll holdup in Akron, O. . . . Six trolley line poles in Brookline Blvd., called a hazard to motorists, are going to be taken out . . . Aliquippa is going to get a million-dollar shopping center on Broadhead Rd. at Mill St..

William Dickson, 17, of Beaver Falls, was rescued in Allegheny River, after a spat with his girl . . . Joseph Evagues, 36, of Denniston Ave., Swissvale, attempted to hold up a restaurant on Fifth Ave. and told police he did it because he wanted to get into jail. He got 60 days in the County Workhouse . . . 14-year-old boy captured upsetting tombstones in Union Dale Cemetery.

The Hoover Commission's investigation of waste turned up a Navy hoard of 886,000 pounds of canned hamburger —enough to last 60 years— and 812,000 gallons of ketchup to go with them— about a gallon for each hamburger. The Navy has been ordered to "eat" the surplus . . . The Rev. F. X. Foley, native of Lawrenceville, is celebrating 25 years as a priest. He is pastor now of St. Mary's Church, Kittanning.

Ten men overcome by fumes in Isabella mine near Brownsville—all okay now . . . That bullet fired by William C. Mueller, 18, of Ross Township, into the leg of Policeman Charles Rieck, struck a nickel and dime he had in his pocket and drove them into his thigh . . . Joan Crawford eloped to Las Vegas with Alfred N. Steele, president of Pepsi Cola. Her fourth marriage.

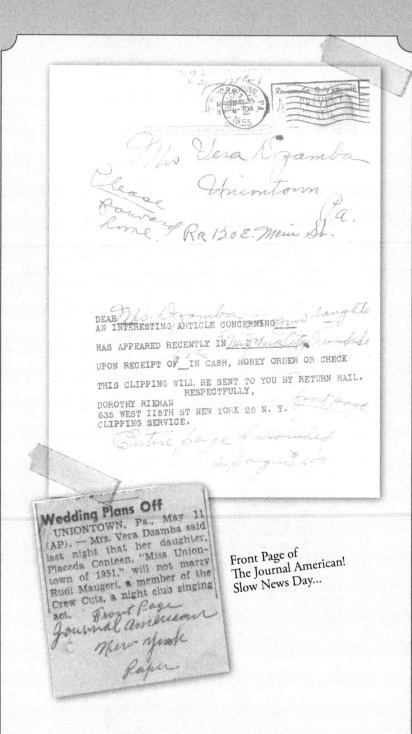

Mrs Vera Dzamba
Uniontown
Pa.
Please forward home. RR 130 E. Main St.

POSTMARKED: UNIONTOWN, PA. MAY 11 1955

DEAR Mrs. Dzamba — your daughter
AN INTERESTING ARTICLE CONCERNING
HAS APPEARED RECENTLY IN New York City newspaper
UPON RECEIPT OF _IN CASH, MONEY ORDER OR CHECK
THIS CLIPPING WILL BE SENT TO YOU BY RETURN MAIL.
RESPECTFULLY,
DOROTHY RIEMAN
635 WEST 115TH ST NEW YORK 25 N. Y.
CLIPPING SERVICE.

Front page
Entire page furnished
5 page $1.00

Wedding Plans Off
UNIONTOWN, Pa., May 11 (AP). — Mrs. Vera Dzamba said last night that her daughter, Placeda Conteen, "Miss Uniontown of 1951," will not marry Rudi Maugeri, a member of the Crew Cuts, a night club singing act.

Front Page
Journal American
New York
Paper

Front Page of
The Journal American!
Slow News Day...

THE PITTSBURGH PRESS

Second Class Mail
At Pittsburgh

v
f
President Jose in Iver
was assassinated last   **WEDNESDAY, MAY 11, 1955**
board.

The Song Had Meaning

'Crew Cut' Dedicates 'Jilted' to Fiancee

Singer Was Married Two Weeks Ago, Uniontown Beauty Queen Discovers

UNIONTOWN, May 11 (Special)—The way her mother explains it, Beauty Queen Placeda Conteen had to call off her marriage to a member of the singing Crew Cuts.

"There wasn't anything else to do," said Mrs. Vera Dzamba.

Turns out that the Canadian singer, Rudi Maugeri, already has a bride.

Twenty - two - year - old Placeda, who was Miss Uniontown of 1951, met Rudi at a Pittsburgh night club a year ago when the Crew Cuts appeared there.

They announced their engagement at the same night spot last December.

Apparently, they planned to marry in June as the Crew Cuts agent had said the singer would be unavailable the week of June 6 because he would be honeymooning.

But it's all over now, said Mrs. Dzamba, who learned that Rudi married another girl about two weeks ago.

"When we heard about it," she said, "I called up to confirm it. Maurgeri said he married somebody else."

Mrs. Dzamba still wasn't convinced, so she called Fred Strauss, manager of the Crew Cuts, at his Cleveland office.

"He confirmed Maurgeri's marriage," she said. "There wasn't anything else to do but call off the wedding."

Mrs. Dzamba said her daughter—a former Pittsburgh nurse who was third-place winner in the 1951 Miss Pennsylvania contest—is now in Florida to avoid publicity over the breakup.

If the jilted miss wants an explanation, she might try to see Rudi in Pittsburgh the week of May 30.

The Crew Cuts are doing a return engagement at the same spot where Rudi and Placeda met.

, *Weds Showgirl*

Nurse Placeda Conteen is girl Rudi first chose

Cindy Brooks has ring—both in picture and from Crew Cut Rudi Maugeri.

'Oh Well—Showbusiness!'

One of Toronto's Crew Cuts, Rudi Maugeri, has broken his publicized engagement to a demure Philadelphia nurse and has secretly married a shapely Las Vegas showgirl.

The whirlwind courtship and marriage 10 days ago of the Sh' Boom boy. _____ _____ came as a shock to his mother in Toronto, who learned of it only last night.

"I can't believe it," his mother gasped, when the news was broken to her. "Oh well, I guess show business is like that."

Fans of the Crew Cuts—one of North America's most popular singing quartets — their friends, and their families were all taken by surprise.

Rudi had been engaged to Placeda Dee Conteen, a Uniontown, Pa., nurse whose only connection with show business had been her election as "Miss Uniontown" in 1951. They were to have been married June 11.

But Fred Strauss, the quartet's agent, said: "They saw it wasn't just going to work out."

The Crew Cuts are on holiday in various parts of the U.S. Rudi, 24, and his bride, 22, are honeymooning in New York after their marriage in Chicago April 28. Bass Ray Perkins, 22, is in Chicago, recovering from a tonsillectomy. His brother Jack, 23, second tenor, is in Oklahoma, and lead tenor, Pat Barrett, 21, is in Kansas.

Mrs. Frank Maugeri, mother of six other children, was flabbergasted at the sudden turn of events.

"I got a Mother's Day telegram from Rudi, but I haven't had a letter in three weeks and he usually writes regularly," she said.

"I still can't believe it . . . But if Mr. Strauss says it's true, I suppose it must be.

"Frankly, I'm disappointed.

"I think they should have

See RUDI, Page 24

Is Engaged To 'Crew-Cut'

_____town, Pa., ___ ___ ___ (AP)—Mrs. Charles Conteen has announced the engagement of her daughter, Placeda Dee Conteen, to Rudi Maugeri, a member of the "Crew-Cuts" vocal quartet.

A date for the wedding has not yet been set. Miss Conteen is a nurse at the Allegheny General Hospital in Pittsburgh. Rudi Maugeri is a son of Mr. and Mrs. Frank Maugeri of Toronto.

This ran in The Tely.

Crew Cuts' line-up has Rudi, front, followed by Ray Perkins, Jack Perkins, Pat Barrett.

Speaks for itself!

RUDI

Continued From Page One

let me know. A mother expects
that . . . I'm all mixed up,
but if he's got the right girl
he has my blessing."

HE DOESN'T KNOW

Arthur Perkins, father of
two of the quartet, and its
former business manager
didn't know what effect the
sudden marriage might have
on the singers.

"I was in Chicago last week
to see Ray, and he didn't say
anything. They certainly are
close-mouthed," he said.

Toronto press agent for the
group, Dave Bossin, said it was
all news to him.

"I thought I would be the
first they'd tell," he said, "but
people in show business are
liable to do anything."

He didn't think the surprise
move would have any effect on
the group. "They've just in-
corporated themselves, w i t h
their New York agent, as Crew
Cuts Inc.," he explained. "I
don't think this will make any
difference."

Father B. F. Ronan, who
started the boys on their singing career when they joined
St. Michael's Cathedral choir
years ago, said the effects of
marriage can be measured in
two ways, "from the religious
point of view and from the
theatrical point of view."

"If it's a good marriage according to his religion, it's
good," he said.

Miss Conteen's mother, Mrs.
Vera Dzamba, said the engagement had been broken off
some weeks ago.

Rudi met his bride while
the group were playing a date
in Las Vegas, Nev., shortly
after his first engagement had
been broken.

WE WERE SHOCKED

Speaking from Uniontown,
Pa., Mrs. Vera Dzamba, Placeda's mother, told The Telegram: "The marriage shocked
all of us. It was the feeling we
got . . . Rudi marrying so soon."

Mrs. Dzamba said there was
no "hard feeling" between
Rudi and Placeda, but admitted
that her daughter had gone to
Florida "for a holiday and a
complete rest."

She said the young couple
first "postponed the wedding
and then decided to call it off.
A few days later we got a call
saying he was going to marry
another girl."

In Toronto last December,
Miss Conteen said she first
met the famous Crew Cuts
when they were playing an engagement in Pittsburgh.

WE MET THEM

"I had bought their records,"
she said, "and when a party
of us went to see them, we
met them after the show."

Miss Conteen decided at
that time to continue with her
nursing duties at the Alle-
ghany General Hospital, in
Pittsburgh, until she and Rudi
were married.

June 11, 1955: The Beach

On the weekends, we went to the beach. For me, the beach was the most relaxing place on earth. So soothing; a calm would come over me just looking at the beautiful water, the sky, the white clouds. I could sit and read and think for hours. I hated to leave it. I felt it was healing me.

We met some fellas there who were the first real friends we made in Florida. They lived near us, and they also had two cars, and would loan us a car. We never took advantage, borrowing only when really necessary.

The beautiful morning of Saturday, June 11th was my very sad wedding day. I went to my favorite place on the beach, with a copy of *Gone With The Wind* that I hoped would hold my interest and keep the tears from falling.

I sat there under the completely baby-blue cloudless sky, meeting the green water watching the frothy surf running on the snowy-looking sand and my favorite bird, the sand piper. An awesome sight. I kept telling myself, I can get through this day, I can move on, I can!

But after every four or five pages I'd find my mind wandering. I'd be getting into my beautiful gown now, the hairdresser would be securing the veil in my hair, I'd be switching my engagement ring from the left to the right hand. My bouquet – white roses, a few gardenias, and purple heather. So beautiful!

I would look at my watch and imagine what should have been happening. This was a painful journey through what was supposed to have been the greatest and happiest day of my life. The life before my near-perfect world evaporated like a puff of smoke and I ran. How silly of me to imagine that a wonderful book could have saved me from dreaming about my wedding day.

Evening of June 11th

We had a light dinner and two bottles of wine, and went to bed knowing that the next day would be difficult, too. After Mo fell asleep, I went out on the screened porch and sat. I was up all night, reflecting back on New Year's Day, 1950; that day when I'd been so looking forward to my life, moving into what I'd been sure would be my favorite decade.

July 1955: A Pretty Patient

Work was going very well. I was slowly adjusting to the climate, but still was very tired at the end of the day. I did work overtime and some extra shifts, if they were short-staffed. It was really more for me. Keeping busy and going to the beach was my therapy.

I had a very pretty patient, a head stewardess for National Airlines (they flew the first jet service in the U.S.A. on December 10th, 1958).

She was at the hospital for two weeks, and we became very friendly. The captains, co-pilots and a lot of the crew dropped by to visit her every day. I enjoyed meeting them and joking with them. They said I should interview for the airlines, since they loved having nurses as stewardesses. They all said I would easily pass the interviews and exams. They made it seem so glamorous.

I told my roommates that I was thinking of doing this. Mo thought she would be interested also. We would still live with Jo and Rose Marie whenever we were in Miami. We arranged for interviews, and then testing. One evening after dinner, we stopped at the drug store to get a few things. I heard Rose Marie say to Jo, "Come here and look at this," so I went too, and she was holding a magazine. They really didn't want me to see it. There was a picture of Rudi and one of the new wife, but there was also a story with it, and it had not only my name, but also an ugly picture and lies.

I was so hurt and angry. We left immediately and as soon as I got home, I called my mother. It was about 8:15 P.M. and she answered. "Mom have you sent me every article about me and Rudi that has appeared in papers or magazines? I'm referring to the nasty ones, because I just found one, it was filled with lies, very upsetting. Look, you and Charlie have been wonderful, I know you are trying to shield me, but I don't want that, I have to know everything in order to go forward, I want you to send me everything tomorrow, please." After I hung up, I sat down and wrote a letter to Fred S., the Crew-Cuts manager.

I gave no interviews, even though reporters continued to contact my mother to ask for interviews. My answer was "no," because I didn't want to harm the other guys, Johnnie, Pat, and Ray; I cared too much for them. Fred sent me a condescending letter about two months later. But now that I was receiving some of the newspaper clippings and magazines, seeing the lies that Fred the manager was telling about me, I was shocked. I wasn't a show business person, true, but I understood the workings of show business very well. We weren't of a different religion; Rudi and I were both Catholics. I understood Fred's position; he was protecting his "meal ticket." But lies were never necessary. He was thrilled that I'd kept quiet and sort of ridden off into the sunset. He could have simply said, "Rudi decided to marry someone else. I can't say anything more."

The lie that crushed me was the one he gave to all the papers, that Rudi and I had broken up in February and he'd met this women in March. February was probably our best month and we didn't break up 'till April, and the phone call.

I could have picked up a phone any time, called the papers and magazines, and exposed these and the other lies. But I didn't. At times I thought I should have, but it was over and I wasn't into revenge.

Florida, Summer 1955: The Psychic

I overheard some patients talking about a fortune teller who was supposed to be so fantastic that people were waiting in line to get an appointment. I asked them a lot questions, and decided that I'd go for a reading. Relatives and friends still insisted that Rudi and I would someday be together. Maybe the fortune teller could clear that up. Two of my roommates were interested too, so I called for three appointments. We had to wait nearly a month to get in, and we borrowed a car to get there.

"Let me go first, because you might let something slip about me, and I don't want her to know anything," I asked my friends. They agreed, and after a fifteen minute wait, I was in. The fortune teller was at a table in a dimly-lit dining room, and invited me to sit at her right. I couldn't really tell her age, as she had on a scarf and glasses. I was looking for a crystal ball, but there wasn't one. I had never done this before, and was beginning to wonder why I'd come. As I sat down, she gently touched my hand and I smiled. She stared at me silently for what seemed like an uncomfortably long time, maybe two or three minutes. Finally, she spoke.

"You have a beautiful smile on a pretty face, but the saddest eyes. You have been deeply hurt by a divorce or a broken relationship. You are very devoted to your work, and like to lose yourself in it so you can't think about what has happened." She spoke faster as she laid out the Tarot cards. "I can see you moving in a few months …"

I tried to show no emotion, determined not to help her out, although so far she was pretty much on target. But finally, I had to ask my question.

"The person who has brought me so much sorrow, will I be with him again someday?"

She looked directly into my eyes. "No, but you will find happiness again, and, in time, a true love."

I was shocked, I felt paralyzed. I hadn't realized how much I was expecting a "yes." I could feel tears again rolling down my cheeks to my chin, and then falling, but I couldn't move my hands to wipe them away. I asked what she meant by "in time"; three months, six months, a year?

Her reply was a shocker. "Three to five years."

I said that he was a very successful person, would this last? No, this success would not last and he would have a hard time finding true happiness. After a few more questions, my time was up. As I walked to the door she said, "You will find happiness." I added that he was an entertainer.

She said, "Yes, I know, and he has lost his lucky charm."

At first I didn't believe her; I guess I didn't want to. It took me a couple of days of serious thinking before I realized that it really was time to move on. It had been nearly five months since my world as

I knew it had shattered. No more tears. I would go out and start to date.

Chapter Ten

MOVING ON

CHAPTER 10: MOVING ON

Meeting Damon

The last two or three Saturdays, my roommates had been going to the cocktail lounge in the hotel where we had stayed. We knew people there, and it was fun and safe. I was usually working, and certainly hadn't been ready to date. So, even when they started telling me about this unbelievably handsome First Lieutenant in the Air Force they wanted me to meet, I hadn't been interested.

Mo and Jo were dating two other very nice First Lieutenants, his buddies. They had told him about me. Now I was ready to meet him. I would go with them this coming Saturday night. On Friday, I bought a new dress. Saturday, I had my hair colored and cut, and then spent a few hours on the beach reviving my tan. This was the new me. I wasn't as sure of myself as I pretended to be.

When Mo's date George called her on Thursday from Hurlburt Airfield, Fort Walton Beach, Florida, she told him to bring Damon. They were going to meet the "mystery" roommate.

When we walked into the bar of the cocktail lounge they were sitting there, except for one tall fellow also in uniform, his back to us. They must have said something, because he turned around and walked toward us. He shook my hand and said, "Hi, Plus, I'm Damon," then acknowledged the other girls. "What can I get you to drink?"

"Whatever you have will be fine."

As he walked away, I said, "He's the most gorgeous man I have ever seen, including movie stars." He had big, blue eyes and a wonderful smile.

We sat down at a table and the other fellows came over. There were "hello" kisses and greetings. I was really smiling, and it wasn't fake. I was thinking, he's too good to be true, there must be something wrong, but there wasn't. We danced, walked on the beach, went to Wolfie's for sandwiches, and before we girls got in the cab to go back to Coral Gables, it was about two in the morning, and they were coming to our house at nine for breakfast. We'd spend a couple hours on the beach together before they flew back to their base. It was the nicest weekend I'd had in over five months, and we planned a trip to the base to visit them.

One weekend, my friends Mo, Ann, and I left Coral Gables on a Friday after work. It was raining and just getting dark, and we were speeding when the red and blue lights started flashing in back of us. The officer was very nice; he said it was very slippery, that we should be careful, and told us we were going thirty miles over the speed limit before letting us go.

Ten minutes later, going about five or ten miles over the limit, we hydroplaned and went over an embankment. We were so very lucky, just shaken and a little bruised. I remember the lights of the ambulance and police cars flashing as they helped us out of the car into the driving rain. Several people stopped to see if we needed help before the nice policeman returned – only he wasn't so nice now, hands on his hips, wanting to say "I told you so," insisting we get in the ambulance. He did not win that argument. It was really uncanny how we escaped serious injuries. They examined the car, which looked terrible but was drivable, and we went slowly and quietly back to Miami. We were stopped about an hour later for driving without a license plate, because our bumper was in the trunk.

We arrived home about one in the morning. We scared the hell out of our roommates, Jo and Marie, who were awakened by a noisy car pulling into the driveway, and then voices whispering and someone trying to get in the back door.

As we entered our bedroom, their room across from ours was dark. We thought we should wake them to tell them of our harrowing experience. They weren't in their beds. Where could they be at this hour? They were hiding in the closet, and finally came out when they recognized our voices. They'd armed themselves with hangers and shoes.

We had already called Damon and George from a pay phone at a gas station shortly after the accident. They were shocked by our news, but we said we had to get back to Miami before the car expired, we were okay if shaken, would tell them all about it at a later time, but we obviously wouldn't be there. We promised to call as soon as we arrived home.

Hurlburt Field, Fla.
23 August 1955

Dear Plus —

    My trip to Miami
seems like a dream, now
that I am back in this
"out of it" place. You certainly made the trip
enjoyable for me.

    From what I gather
you weren't too happy with
my giving Mike your phone
number. I definitely was
not trying to "test" you

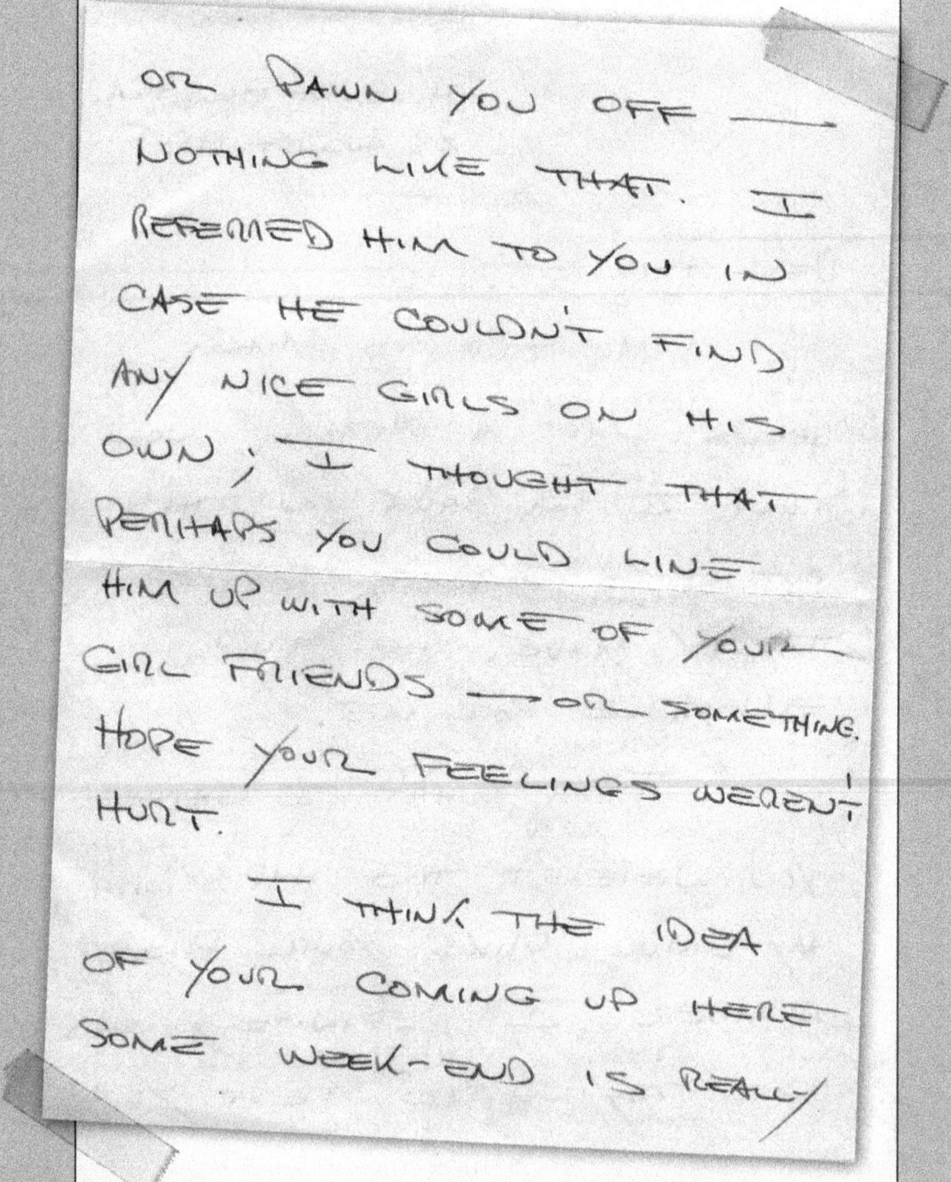

OR PAWN YOU OFF —
NOTHING LIKE THAT. I
REFERRED HIM TO YOU IN
CASE HE COULDN'T FIND
ANY NICE GIRLS ON HIS
OWN; I THOUGHT THAT
PERHAPS YOU COULD LINE
HIM UP WITH SOME OF YOUR
GIRL FRIENDS — OR SOMETHING.
HOPE YOUR FEELINGS WEREN'T
HURT.

I THINK THE IDEA
OF YOUR COMING UP HERE
SOME WEEK-END IS REALLY

TREMENDOUS. COULD YOU
MAKE IT UP ON THE LABOR
DAY WEEK-END (3,4 & 5 SEPTEMBER)?
GEORGE WOULD LIKE TO SEE
MO; MIKE, JO; AND IT
GOES WITHOUT SAYING THAT
I WOULD LIKE TO SEE YOU,
PLUS. WE COULD HAVE A
BLAST!

I AM TRYING TO
WORK A DEAL WITH OPERATIONS
TO GET ON A FLIGHT TO
MIAMI THIS WEEK-END. SURE
WOULD LOVE TO BE WITH

YOU AGAIN. MAYBE THIS TIME YOU COULD SHOW ME AROUND MIAMI. WHAT DO YOU SAY?

WELL, HONEY, PLAY IT COOL AND BE A GOOD GAL. HOPE TO SEE YOU REAL SOON.

LOVE,

DAMON

19 September 1955

My Dearest Dee,

Although I have not heard from you since late last night, I trust you have recovered from your frightening experience. I certainly hope so anyway, darling. After talking to you, I had nothing but "night mares" all night. It really shook me up, but at the same time I was very thankful that it wasn't worse. Honey, if anything serious happened to you I would go insane, I love you so terribly much.

George, Mike and I are

GOING TO CALL YOU THIS EVENING.
CERTAINLY HOPE WE CAN GET IN
TOUCH WITH YOU.

NO DOUBT YOUR ACCIDENT
HAS DISCOURAGED YOUR COMING
UP THIS WEEK. WELL, HONEY,
WE BOYS ARE WORKING HARD ON
LINING UP A FLIGHT TO MIAMI
THIS WEEK-END. I'M ALMOST
POSITIVE WE WILL BE ABLE TO
ARRANGE IT.

HONEY, I RECEIVED A LETTER
FROM G.E. THE OTHER DAY STATING
THAT, DUE TO A COMPANY-WIDE
RAISE IN WAGES, MY SALARY WILL
BE $422 INSTEAD OF $410. I
KNOW THAT THIS IS PEANUTS COMPARED

TO WHAT RUDY MAKES, BUT I
FEEL THAT WE CAN LIVE ON
IT. NEXT AUGUST I WILL
BE ELIGIBLE FOR ANOTHER
RAISE, SO WE SHOULDN'T STARVE
EVEN IF WE DO START ON
OUR FAMILY THE FIRST YEAR.
WHAT DO YOU THINK?

IN YOUR LAST TWO LETTERS
YOU MADE THE COMMENT TO
THE EFFECT THAT YOU HOPED
YOUR LETTERS DIDN'T BORE ME.
MY DARLING, IF YOU GAVE ME
NOTHING BUT A WEATHER REPORT
I WOULD <u>NOT</u> BE BORED. I
LOVE YOU, HONEY, SO YOU COULDN'T
BORE ME IF YOU TRIED.

TODAY, PICHELMAYER AND
I PLAYED HOOKEY AND WENT
TO THE BEACH. BOTH OF US
GOT FAIRLY WELL BAKED. SURE
HOPE I DON'T PEEL, AS I
WANT TO HAVE A GOOD FLORIDA
TAN WHEN I ARRIVE IN SPRING
HILL. THEY WON'T BELIEVE THAT
I WAS IN FLORIDA ALL SUMMER
IF I AM PALE.

CERTAINLY HOPE YOU STAY
OUT OF ACCIDENTS IN THE FUTURE.
I LOVE YOU AND MISS YOU
TERRIBLY MUCH.

ALL MY LOVE,
DAMON

P.S. GIVE MY REGARDS TO MO & ANN. HOPE
THEY HAVE RECOVERED TOO.

Moe and I

Fun at Hurlburt Airforce Base

Fort Walton Beach, Florida

October 1955: Moving On

October was starting our sixth month in Florida and we weren't sure what we wanted to do.

Damon wrote after reading the morning paper about the tragic United Airlines accident, "It made me feel good that I was instrumental in your staying out of the stewardess position. Certainly hope that you don't get any crazy notions to try it. I kinda like you and would like to see you stay alive."

Mo had decided she no longer was interested in being a stewardess. Her romance with her dashing First Lieutenant was getting quite serious, and she was very happy. Jo was still dating Ron, a really nice guy. These two fellows were still in the Air Force and thought we should come to Fort Walton Beach to work.

Damon had been discharged and was on his way back to Kansas to be an engineer at General Electric in Ohio. He wanted to get married, after returning home to break the news to his folks and getting settled in his job. I was thinking of going back to Uniontown, and so was Marie. Mo and Jo left in October.

Ann wanted me to come to New York City, saying that we could share an apartment. We certainly had many hospitals to choose from, and could almost be assured of getting any position we wanted. I promised her that I'd think seriously about this move.

November 1955: Going Home

I felt the need to go home and work at Uniontown Hospital. I really had to figure out what I was going to do with my life. I knew nursing was my first love, and was thinking about possibly continuing my education.

In the fall of 1955, I was home for a few weeks, and I wrote to Damon that we both should try dating other people. I felt I liked him very much, but did I really love him? Was this romance a rebound? I also did not want another long-distance relationship. As stupid as it was, I still had some feelings for Rudi. Damon – what a wonderful guy some girl would be getting, but it was not for me at this time.

Jerry, the fellow I had been dating when I met Rudi, called. He had kept in touch with my mother by an occasional note or phone call to see how I was doing. He told me he was getting used to seeing my name or pictures in the Pittsburgh papers. Then came the day when he opened the paper to see me on the front page, smiling, but the headline read "Singer Jilts Beauty." He thought he would wait a while before contacting me.

When I came back to Uniontown, everyone treated me as if I had just been away and now welcome back. After all the publicity, no questions, just kindness; that's the kind of people I grew up with and went to school with. I was so lucky. The newspaper heard I was returning home, and they asked my mother if they could write a small article, Welcome Back. "No, thank you," I said. "I just want to come back quietly. I've had enough publicity to last me a lifetime."

I went to work at Uniontown Hospital, working the night shift, my choice. I knew it well – I'd had my tonsils taken out there when I was seven. As a nine-year-old, I had sat by my mother's bedside for a week, holding her hand as she slept peacefully. I did not understand why she wouldn't respond when I kissed her or called her. She was in a coma. She had gotten dizzy when she was shopping and had fallen down a flight of stairs. Her diagnosis was a fractured skull. Children under fourteen were not allowed to visit, but I would sit in the lobby for hours. She was in a private room, and in that wing my dad had somehow gotten permission to bring me to her room for an hour or so each day. The nurses pretended they didn't see, while also being very kind to me. I loved them and wanted to be just like them.

In late spring, when I was fifteen, I lied about my age and filled out an application to be a nurse's aide at this wonderful hospital. You had to be sixteen. By the end of the summer, I knew as I always had that I wanted to be a nurse.

Christmas 1955: Looking Back

I had been working nights for about six weeks now, so I felt it was certainly fair to work my favorite holiday. Last Christmas, Rudi and I were already planning what our first Christmas as "Mr. and Mrs. M," as he called us, would be like.

His schedule permitting, we would spend our first Christmas with my family this year. If we could not get home, we would get a tiny Christmas tree for our hotel room and buy ornaments in a five and dime store, keep one ornament as a remembrance, and leave the rest for the maid. New Year's Eve and Day, I volunteered to work. How could I do anything else, after the magical New Year's I'd had the previous year?

Jerry came from Pittsburgh on Christmas Day for dinner. Afterwards, he drove me to work and continued on his way back to Pittsburgh. He urged me to come to Pittsburgh for a big New Year's Eve party and dance. He said that many of the old gang from our dating days would be there who wanted to see me. I wanted to see them also. But I knew I wouldn't be good company. I promised to get there in a week or two for a three-day weekend. I would stay with my old roommate, Les, and her husband and son, David. Their door was always open to me.

Getting through these holidays was something I was dreading. But I made it, surrounded by people that cared.

January 1956: Hitting a Stride

The winter was passing quickly. It was a cold, snowy season, and sometimes trudging off at 10:15 at night wasn't all that inviting, but I liked this shift.

I was "floating," working a different floor almost every night as a replacement if someone called in sick or had time off. I got to know a lot more of the members of the staff.

In January, I was given my own floor. It was in the Women's Ward, which was very large. There were a few private rooms, and some semi-private. I had a nurse's aide and a student nurse to help me, and sometimes a grad. We'd grab a fifteen-minute break at about 3:00 A.M. if everything was calm. We would admit patients from the ER, and also from the OR (from emergency surgery). We did not have recovery rooms yet, or Intensive Care. Nights paid a few dollars more. My paycheck was $112.50, plus $5.40 (nights) every two weeks. Allegheny General paid only $235 a month, although you did get a free meal, two weeks paid vacation and two weeks sick time.

In Miami, no one recognized me or cared who Miss Uniontown, 2nd runner up to Miss Pennsylvania, was. In Uniontown, people did remember, and they also remembered the "almost" celebrity wedding. It was a big deal in a small town.

I was now caring for friends or someone in their family. But strangers remembered the name written on my name pin. Curious strangers asked me a few questions. I did learn to be comfortable with these questions.

One thing I did come to terms with was why I'd just had to run away. I now realized that it would be the last time I would ever run away from anything in my life. I really felt that now I could face whatever happened, and deal with it. After all, every night I was taking care of people who had so much more to face, and they couldn't run. A broken heart can mend. I was lucky, and I felt I was really starting to heal.

Little did I know what a great help my nursing career would be for me at this time. You can't allow your mind to wander too much when you're taking care of seriously ill people who need your full attention. And, wherever you work, there always seems to be a shortage of nurses, so you are very busy, working weekends, holidays, all different shifts.

Nurses are very special people. You must love people to be a good nurse. I guess you would say you have to be a "people person." The joy and love you get back from some of the patients and their families are at times overwhelmingly rewarding. I am so glad I am a nurse, and a damn good one too.

February 1956: Jerry's Letter

At this time, I met a pretty student nurse, Carol, and introduced her to Jerry's closest friend, John. The four of us would double date. It was great playing Cupid; after her graduation, they got married.

I was dating both Jerry and Earl, who was in the Air Force. I heard from him frequently, but he couldn't get home too often. They were both terrific fellows whom I had known for a long time. Each of them knew I was seeing the other guy, and that I wasn't interested in a serious involvement. Neither of them was thrilled with this arrangement, but said they understood.

It was at this time that I heard from a mutual friend that Rudi's marriage was basically over. I guess I wasn't really surprised, but tried not to think about it.

I was getting to a good place in my life, dating and enjoying being with old friends. I liked my job, and my mother loved having me home. But, deep down, I knew that I would not be staying in Uniontown or Pittsburgh. Was it because I had so many memories there, many good ones, but were the sad ones overpowering the good ones? I wasn't sure.

I consider both of these places my hometown. I was born in Pittsburgh, moved to Uniontown when I was six years old, went to seventh and eighth grade at St. Peters in Pittsburgh, back to

Uniontown for high school, then to Pittsburgh for almost four years after that. When someone asked me where I was from, I always said both places. The steel mills and the coal mines; I was very proud of both.

L. P. STIMMLER, Agent

1501 UNION NATIONAL BANK BUILDING

PITTSBURGH 22, PA.

February 28, 1956

Hello Little One:

Nice to know that I may see my urchin friends from Union-town again this week. In fact — I'm looking forward to it.

I talked to Jouie after I called you last night. He came up with a wonderful idea — "why doesn't he drive everyone back to Uniontown on Sunday?" I had to admit the idea had merit — in fact I would have suggested it but he saved me the trouble. Good boy!

So, if nothing else — you're

L. P. STIMMLER, Agent
1501 UNION NATIONAL BANK BUILDING
PITTSBURGH 22, PA.

at least guaranteed a ride home.

I was toying with the idea of holding you in Pittsburgh, as hostage, in return for the family jewels but Charlie would probably tell me that I already had the family jewel in my possession. I don't doubt that he'd probably even subsidize your upkeep just to be rid of ya so I can't make any loot on that deal. Seriously - I am looking forward to seeing you again. Plus even if it is only from Thursday til Monday - we'll have a good time

L. P. STIMMLER, Agent

1501 UNION NATIONAL BANK BUILDING

PITTSBURGH 22, PA.

anyway.

While talking to your mother before she called you to the 'phone last evening, she told me that you had been bothered with insomnia for the last couple days. Please - please don't lose any sleep - you'll see me again - I'll be around for awhile. Of course this probably sounds presumptuous on my part I know - but then - consider the source.

I hope Bobbie decides to come in along - it would take all the pleasure out of Louie driving back! (if he does it - that is) Of course he'll still

CAPITAL STOCK

Standard protection

COMPANY INSURANCE

L. P. STIMMLER, Agent

1501 UNION NATIONAL BANK BUILDING

PITTSBURGH 22, PA.

drive you (and if she comes, Carol)
back, but you know the trip
would be much more pleasant
for him if he had the proper
feminine company. Please convey
my complements to Charlie. He has
a nice niece. ~~to me~~ Lots of fun.

I picked up 60⁰⁰ from my
insurance company as a result of
the accident — we'll at least have
something to drink on over the
weekend. I've been thinking —
seeing as I was an innocent
bystander in this claim — I'm
also entitled to a small
settlement, too. If this

L. P. STIMMLER, Agent

1501 UNION NATIONAL BANK BUILDING

PITTSBURGH 22, PA.

should come to pass; we'll
either blow it in in Uniontown
or New York — but we'll get some
fun out of the mishap, anyway.

I guess that's it for now —
Shortie — see you Thursday —

Love,

Kerry

23 March 56

Hi ya Beautiful,

You know you told me a big fib on the telephone last time I talked to you. I never did get that letter but sure have been lookin for it. Decided not to be stubborn any longer tho. Anyway I haven't been able to check the mail for the last week or so, been out on this trip since Sunday. So far its Delaware to Newfoundland to England and back to Iceland. It's about 3 A.M. Iceland time right now and 11 P.M. your time. My student and I are sitting here waiting for a room. This whole deal is a Strategic Air Command movement and from here we're going to Detroit to Reno, Hunter and back to Charleston. It could be a real nice trip but I don't care much for the Aircraft Commander. He is one big pain in the you know where. I missed my E.T.A. into Prestwick Scotland by 3 minutes after a 12 hour flight over the Atlantic which for several people is a real good E.T.A. Not him tho. He had to say something about it. Also we took off from England 20 hours early and only had about 15 hours there. Usually we get at least 24 hours at a turn-around station. Do I sound like I'm crying the blues?? Tough of my problems huuh? So, after all that I guess we'll be back in Charleston in about four more days.

Hey honey, I wanted to ask you about that wedding next month. You know — all the details. Where is it?? How many days. When is it and etc. Also, can I come too?? No kidding that would be a real nice vacation for me. Probably could get a week if I asked real nice. I could drive up instead of fly and then we could use my car to go from H'town. I'm not sure, I think you said it was in Ohio. I'm not sure I could swing the deal but if you would like me to I would try real hard.

How have things been going for you? Are you still working at the hospital? How bout your love life? Hope you haven't progressed too far along these lines. Still think it's about time we got hitched.

Don't know much more to say right now "sweets". Could tell you all about my "xciting" (joke) life in M.A.T.S. but you'd gotta sleep on that. We did lose an engine this time tho. Big deal with one cargo. Looks funny as heck to see the prop standing still when it should be spinning. They come out and meet you in a rescue plane and escort you back to the field with all the honors. By that I mean that they have a half dozen fire trucks and a couple "meat wagons" escort you down the runway. That was the third time tho and the excitement is all gone. First two were burning when we hit the dock. This one just got tired and quit. Like I said before — big deal.

Think I'll close up shop for this morning and wait till I hear from you. Don't forget to write.

Love ya. E

(over)

P.S. the picture was taken New Years eve in our living room just before our "blast" at the club. Had it in my letter box and been meaning to send it for a couple weeks.

3 April 56

Dear Plus,

It's been a couple of days since I
rec'd your last letter and finally now that
I do get around to answering it I am
doing what has become the usual thing.
Sitting on an airplane on the way to Thule.
This time tho' it's kind of a special flight
'cause I'm going as a replacement navigator
for a boy that got sick in McGuire,
New Jersey. Soo — if he is ok. by the time
I get there I might just turn around and
come back home. That's MATS for you tho.
You never know what's happening until it
happens. Yesterday this time I had no idea that
I would be going on this flight.

Please don't feel bad about me not being
able to come to the wedding. If I had known
the details I'm sure I would never have
given it a thought. I thought it was going
to be another big old "blast" like Steve and
Ann's wedding and figured I could probably
crash the party. So please disregard my
forwardness in asking you to let me
come.. OK?? It really sounds nice tho
honey and if you can sneak a picture all

by your lonesome I would appreciate it
"mightily." Wanta have some idea of what you
are gonna look like when we get around
to "tying the knot." Ha..!! I really wouldn't
need a picture to serve that purpose tho.
Seems to me that a few years back I
imagined something like that many times.
I sure am grateful to someone or something that we didn't do as I wanted to
then tho. When I think about it I
think I must have been clean out of
my mind. I could never have had
what I have or been what I am
today and neither could you. But in
another way, we would probably have
had a couple of kids (both boys) and
that part I would have liked very
much. Do I sound silly? Probably
so. One thing I could never promise is
that the same thing wouldn't happen to
me next time I see you. Which, by
the way, had better be pretty damned
soon! You know, after you go to New
York it will be quite simple for me to
get over to see you from McGuire and
we have a flight going there there every

day. I'm still hoping that I'll be able to come to U'town the last week in April since you are all tied up the first half of the month. That be ok with you??

My buddy and I bought a boat last week and I've been able to log a couple more hours of skiing time over the week-end. It's a pretty nice looking outfit. It's a 14 foot runabout with a 25 h.p. Evinrude outboard. Has a windshield, steering wheel, remote controls and a speedometer for extras. So far we've only been able to get it up to 31 m.p.h. but I sure hope to do a little better when we get the engine tuned just right. It's still plenty fast for the skis tho. When are you gonna come down and ski with me? Charleston is really beautiful this time of the year. temp. is about 80° and there must be a million flowers blooming. Maybe even more than that.

Well 'chicken', I guess I'll drop this off in Mc Guire when we land so I had better start closing up shop. Let me quote the last line of your letter. "I'll write more later" – Of course I realize you didn't say how much later but no kiddin' please don't wait so long next time. I know you are

gonna be real busy but, aren't we all—
Huh?! Be "good" and have a ball at the
wedding.

Love ya,
Paul

P.S. Quite a crack-up in Pitts. wasn't
it?

March 1956: The Journal

One weekend in March, the weather turned nasty. I was off and had planned on going to Pittsburgh, but decided that staying home would be wiser.

My mom brought up a very large box of memorabilia from my high school days, and suggested that reading through it (and maybe getting rid of some of it) might occupy some of my time. Since it was just high school stuff and some contest clippings, she figured it would bring back harmless, happy memories. We were coming up on the one-year anniversary of the phone call which we no longer talked about, but which I knew we'd all be thinking of.

Good idea! Midway through the box, I found my high school and nursing school journal that I'd started on New Year's Day, 1950, and stopped my senior year at A.G.H. This journal tells of very important happy days from my special decade.

My former roommate, Mo, married her dashing first lieutenant, George, the last Saturday in March at Beaver Falls, Pennsylvania. It was a lovely wedding. They were both so happy, you were just happy to be in their presence.

April 1956: Ceatta and Don's Wedding

I was off to Kent State University where I was going to be maid of honor in my cousin Ceatta's wedding. Don and Ceatta were seniors, and so fond of their priest and church there, as well as their school and friends, they'd decided that this was where they wanted to be married.

The wedding party was big. The baby blue cocktail dress I was wearing was stunning. We would be leaving from the sorority house.

I worked Thursday night and was on my way to Kent, Ohio, by 9:30 Friday morning. That afternoon Ceatta had some errands to do and suggested I take a nap so that I would be refreshed for the rehearsal party.

I woke from my nap, hearing about six girls discussing me in whispers:

"Is she the one that broke her engagement to the Crew-Cut?"

"Well, I think she was jilted."

"Oh, no!" said another.

"Ceatta was supposed to be in her wedding last year. I've met her, she is very nice."

"I haven't met her yet. Is she beautiful, like her cousin says?"

"She's very pretty, she was almost Miss Pennsylvania."

Another girl asked, "Then why did he jilt her?"

"Oh, I don't know, but please don't ask her."

I stayed very still until they moved on. This weekend was the one-year anniversary. Would people ever stop talking?

The morning of the wedding, we had to wrap the bride in sheets to get her into the limo. It was April 7th, and it was snowing.

The reception was so much fun. In the receiving line this handsome, blue-eyed blond fellow introduced himself as sort of a new relative. He was Paul, the groom's half brother. They didn't resemble each other. Don had dark hair and dark eyes. We had a fun time together, and did date after the wedding.

A few weeks after the wedding, while boosting a patient up in bed, I felt a pain on my right side. It was very intense momentarily, and then, as it was fading, it seemed to travel to my upper abdominal wall.

When I got home, I was somewhat nauseated. I went directly to bed, no breakfast upon arising. Later in the afternoon, I felt some pain in my right side, more nausea, and had a slight fever. Any nurse could make the diagnosis.

I was off this night and had hoped to go to Pittsburgh to see Jerry, but that plan was not going to happen. It was a trip to the E.R. After blood tests, I was examined by attending Dr. L. Appendicitis of course. I was allowed to go home for my personal things and return for a surgery early in the morning. I was told that my appendix was close to rupturing. I was quite sick for a few days, and was in the hospital for a week. The newspaper ran a small article, saying I was recuperating after surgery. I did receive many cards and notes, plus flowers.

May 1956: Recouping

I went to Lorain, Ohio to visit family and stay with my Aunt Margaret and her little girl, Sharon. I was on sick leave, and planning a trip to New York to visit Ann, who had just arrived there and was looking at apartments. I was pretty sure that New York City was my next home. I did not know for how long! I had loved it when I had been there five years earlier.

Rudi's marriage was now in the divorce court. It had only lasted a matter of months.

Paul, who lived in Solan, about 45 minutes from Lorain, came to visit and brought a friend for Margaret. We had a nice time double dating.

I was also visiting with my friend P.K., who lived less than an hour away in Cleveland. She and Ray the Crew-Cut were dating. Ray and I had remained close friends. He told me how sorry he was that Rudi had hurt me like he had. He had felt so sure that Rudi loved me so much that he would never do anything like that. We called each other "cousin" and kept in touch.

One of the newspaper headlines read, "She (me) was like a little sister to the other Crew-Cuts." I guess that was true.

Jerry kept in touch by mail and a weekly phone call. He wrote the best letters; long, funny, and his vocabulary was superb. He wanted me to stop in Pittsburgh for three or four days on my way home from Ohio.

The previous fall, I had mentioned to him that my fairly new friend, Ann, wanted me to move to New York. We were corresponding while I was in Florida, and he as well as Damon didn't want me to be a stewardess. He wasn't too keen on my moving to New York, either. Now I was sure I was going for two weeks, and then probably home for a month or two before the real move. I thought I would tell him when I saw him in Pittsburgh.

Earl would be happy, because he was stationed at McGuire Air Base in New Jersey, and envisioned many trips to the city. He would become a captain for United Airlines.

Chapter Eleven

A NEW CHAPTER: NEW YORK CITY

CHAPTER 11: A NEW CHAPTER, NEW YORK CITY

June 1956: The City

I flew to New York the end of May, for ten days. Ann had started working at a small, private hospital on the East Side and was staying at a friend's apartment. She had found us a small, beautiful sublet in the fabulous Schwab House on the West Side. It was very grand, with an impressive lobby and a doorman. It would be ready the first of July and available for at least six months. I think that seeing that apartment sealed the deal.

While I was looking at hospitals and getting applications, I visited with my cousins and went to a Broadway show. We walked up and down 5th Avenue. The subways were crowded, but we rode them so that I could get used to the fast pace. It certainly would be very different from working in Pittsburgh and Florida. This city was a little scary, but so electrifying.

My mother had lived in New York with her cousins as a young girl for a short time. She knew how captivating this city could be. She thought that I should go and "maybe in six months you'll get it out of your system."

I learned from my friends that Rudi's divorce was going to be final in Chicago this month. Crew-Cut Pat was being married this month. The Crew-Cuts were still at the top of their popularity.

I came back to Uniontown June 6th, went back to work, and felt fine.

Jerry and a friend came the first weekend I was home. My aunt came from Ohio, and we went to a beautiful formal at the Country Club.

July and August 1956: Three Rivers Inn

Time was going very quickly, I had handed in my resignation. I really liked my job, and I gave them a month to replace me. As sad as I was to be leaving, I felt very confident I was making the right decision.

I moved to New York City on July 10th. Ann was already making new friends and plans for us.

I had some plans, too, and later that month we drove upstate to Three Rivers Inn. Ray had planned a visit, which I'd made him promise not to tell anyone about, except his brother, John. I would not be going to the show. Our friendship was strictly platonic. Ann and I had a great weekend, but it was strange knowing that Rudi was so close by. I hadn't seen him for sixteen months, but I really wasn't ready to.

A good friend.

Ray and I at Three Rivers Inn, NY.

July 1956: Running in Central Park

The first day I went for a walk/run in Central Park was a week after I moved to New York City. I had just finished my first day of work, at the Doctors Hospital in Manhattan. I was doing private duty, and my first patient was a delightful gentleman who had had a heart attack two days earlier. I had decided to do private duty because financially it was more lucrative than floor duty or doing a specialty.

I couldn't get my roommate to walk in the park with me, so I went alone. After running for a while, I decided to walk, then sat down on a bench and really started to think about my future here, but also about my past. I was in the greatest city in the world. Now how could I learn and appreciate all it had to offer?

I felt as though I was off to a good start. The apartment was small, but adequate for Ann and me. We were working in a very interesting hospital with many celebrities for patients.

I promised myself to take advantage of Broadway, which I knew I would love. My godmother had introduced me to the theater in Pittsburgh when I was ten years old, and going to the theater was still my favorite entertainment. Museums, Carnegie Hall, the Metropolitan Opera; so much to do and to see.

It'd been over a year now, and I was healing slowly but surely. Broken hearts do mend. I wondered if I'd ever fall deeply in love again. I didn't know, but I wasn't looking for it.

Working at Doctors Hospital was a real treat. I looked forward to going to work every morning. Some weeks, I worked all seven days, as long as the patient needed me. I was doing only the day shift, 7 A.M. to 3:30 P.M.

Some of the celebrities and visitors I met, a few I took care of, and many of them I just saw.

President Harry Truman and wife Bess were visiting their daughter, Margaret Daniels, when she had her first baby. The bandleaders, Tommy and Jimmy Dorsey, both had great bands. Dovima, one of the first super models, was my patient. She was married at the time, and she and her husband were so in love. She was tall, beautiful, and sweet.

One of the singers on the Arthur Godfrey Show was there, and she had a few visitors from the show.

Admiral Halsey was a patient of a doctor friend of mine.

I met the opera star, Maria Callas, and spoke with her many times. Her friend, Elsa Maxwell, a well known columnist, was also a patient.

One morning when I got into work, the hospital was buzzing. Marilyn Monroe had been brought in by ambulance. She was quite sick, and her husband, Arthur Miller, sat by her bedside for hours. She recovered in a week or so.

The day Marilyn was being discharged, her hairdresser and makeup person came. The press was outside, trying to get inside, and the ambulance was parked in front for hours. Everyone, including me, waited patiently for the always-late Miss Monroe to exit.

And it was worth the wait. She was wearing a pink sun dress with matching heels, her hair was in a pageboy style, and she was even more breathtakingly beautiful than in her movies.

Living in New York City was everything I thought it would be. Exciting, exciting, exciting.

August 1956: Blind Dates

Ann was dating Donald, a great Irish guy who was a New York detective, and the two of them kept trying to set me up with his best friend. I was leery, because of the two blind dates that Ann had arranged for me when I first arrived. We always double-dated on blind dates, a rule of mine. She had been introduced to this fellow, a friend of a former patient of hers, when she first arrived in NYC. He called one day and asked her to go out to the Latin Quarter for dinner, dancing, and floor show – and could she get a nice girl for his friend? "Oh, yes," she said, her roommate had arrived a few weeks ago.

This sounded like a fun evening. The doorman announced them, but I didn't catch the last name, only "Joe." I opened the door, and was impressed with the fellows smiling back at me. When they heard my name, that momentarily became the topic of conversation on the elevator and out the front door. The doorman was tripping over his own feet to get the door and the car doors. I assumed they had given him a big tip to get so much attention.

We were given more attention when we arrived at the Latin Quarter. We were having a very nice time, and they were fun. The cigarette girl was flirting with my date, but he was giving his attention to only me, so I was even more impressed, as she was in a very short, sexy costume and looked great. When Ann and I went to the ladies room, I said, "These fellows seemed to be very well-known. This is definitely not their first time here."

Back at our table, our dates suggested a trip to Coney Island the next week, describing Nathan's hot dogs and the rides, everything I liked to do. Ann and I had not been to Coney Island, so we agreed to go with them the following week.

We were having dessert and coffee after the spectacular show, when I heard the waiter call my date by his last name. I swear, a light bulb went off in my head. I almost choked on my coffee! Ann was oblivious to what I was coughing about, and Joe was very concerned as I excused myself to go to the ladies room, motioning Ann to come with me.

When I was sure the ladies room attendant would not hear, I asked Ann if she had a clue who we were with. "Two terrific dates," was her answer. I told her that my date was the son of a very well-known Mafia Don. She was surprised, but not concerned.

Being Italian, I knew this had to be my last date with this very nice man. But how was I going to get out of our plans for next week, and also convince Ann that we didn't really want to get involved with these guys?

The remainder of the evening went well. They were perfect gentlemen. When Joe called two days later, I told him I wouldn't be going, because my boyfriend from Pittsburgh was unexpectedly coming to the city. He was not happy about this, but was polite.

The second blind date Ann set me up with was an entertainer from Hollywood. Again we double dated, and it was a nightmare! I was now done, done, done with blind dates. That's why I was so hesitant about this third one, but as the guy was Donald's best friend, I said yes.

I was pleasantly surprised and happy with meeting Lou. He was so very nice, and it didn't hurt that he looked like the actor Victor Mature. We were dating every week but I refused to go steady at first.

Oct 6/56

Dear Plus;

Well cousin here we are back in the fair
city of Pittsburgh. I had a real ball here this week.
John and I have been doing our own cooking
and I think I put on a little weight. If that's
possible. Jo & Arlene & Peggy were almost in
every night and P.K. was down for the week-end.
She told me to tell you she's not going to write
till she gets a letter from you, and her birthday
is on the 16th of this month.

When are you coming to Cleveland? I told
Pat that you were coming the end of Oct. I hope
I was right, because everyone is expecting you.

John gave his girl the ring last week.

4

when we had a few days off. So it looks like
we're going to have another wedding next June.
Have you found a new apt. yet? If so let me
know your new address.

Everybody is in good health now, but Pat
was sick a couple of weeks ago. Well I'm
running out of things to say. Hope I see you real
soon

Your loving cousin

Ray

Cleveland, October 1956: Trust?

I had promised Ray and P.K. that I would come to Cleveland in October for a long weekend, and to see the Crew-Cuts who were appearing at the Supper Club there. I didn't want them to tell Rudi I was coming. They promised, and I think they kept that promise.

I was staying at P.K.'s home. I bought a new outfit before leaving New York. My hair was much longer and blonder now, and I wore a little more make-up. P.K.'s mom and sisters said I looked fabulous, which made me feel great.

I finally felt ready to see Rudi, up close and personal. I was told he was dating someone. I learned that he'd confessed to a friend that he could never call me after the way he'd treated me, so I guess he knew how terrible the time must have been for me.

P.K. and I sat at a ringside table. Oh, how I remembered the first time I had sat at a ringside table at the Copa, with a different friend, when the only expectation we'd had was hearing our favorite two songs. We hadn't even known their names, just thought they had great harmony.

The Crew-Cuts ran out. Pat noticed us first and with a surprised look, gave us a little wave. Rudi saw us and seemed to do a double take when he realized it was me, but being the professional that he was he didn't miss a note…damn it. I do believe I saw a guilty look on his face, or did I just imagine it?

I didn't notice that much change in the routine, but I always thought they were great, so classy, and I still did.

An hour and fifteen minutes later, they were gone. The crowd loved them and demanded an encore, so they came back out and sang "Sh-boom" again.

Rudi and Ray came to the table, and Rudi asked me to come backstage. I went back. Ray and P.K. stayed at the table for a few minutes, but people were coming up to Ray, so they thought they would come backstage and see what was going on between Rudi and me.

Rudi and I went to the dressing room. The other guys had already changed, and gave me a very warm welcome. Rudi got dressed, and asked me to go out for a bite to eat. I agreed, and we told Ray and P.K. that we'd meet back at the club in two hours.

We took a cab to a restaurant in a different part of town that someone at the club suggested to us. I asked if we could sit in a booth. We ordered sandwiches and a glass of red wine. None of the group was much for drinking.

We talked about what the group was doing, and the new music and arrangements he was always involved in. How did I like New York, my work, everything I was up to? We were polite, distant at first, not asking any invasive questions, like people on their first date. Afterwards, I almost wished I'd said something sarcastic, or at least asked more personal questions – but that was never my style, and too much time had passed for that. I didn't have all the answers but I did learn a few things, which I kept to myself.

We were having coffee when he reached across the table, took my hand and said, "I will always remember you. Would you answer a question honestly for me?"

"That's the only way I've ever answered you," I said.

"Could you ever trust me again?"

I thought for a long moment, knowing that my answer could determine the course of my life.

I looked straight into those dark, dreamy, sexy, brown eyes, at the man that I had trusted so deeply, and said, "Trust? No." I grabbed my purse and ran out.

Where was I going? I was in Cleveland, I didn't know my way around this city. He paid the bill and rushed out after me.

We went back to the club, got P.K. and Ray, and they drove us to her home. We all made light, careful conversation.

When Rudi and I got out of the car, he walked me to the door, hugged me and softly whispered, "I still care." He kissed me goodnight like we had never been apart, but it was really goodbye – I never saw him again! But that was fine; reality had finally sunk in, and I was ready to move on. I know that a few of our friends had hoped that this would get us back together, but now that it was truly over, I felt free.

Home for Christmas, 1956

Doing private duty allowed me the freedom to pick how long my time off would be between cases. I made sure the cases that I took in December would be finished a few days before Christmas.

I flew to Lorain, Ohio on the 23rd to my grandmother's. Mom and Charlie had driven in that morning from Uniontown. I was there in time to help decorate the tree, along with a lot of the aunts, uncles, and cousins. There was eggnog and wine, and lots of laughter.

Christmas Eve found the clan at Midnight Mass and then early breakfast at one of the aunt's. It was a very happy holiday. On the

30th I was on the plane, headed back to New York. The next day, I was off shopping for a pair of shoes to go with my new red cocktail dress, for my New Year's Eve date.

Lou gave me a beautiful three-carat diamond ring on New Year's Eve. We made some plans, but I gave the ring back about eight months later. I was so sorry, but I couldn't really make a commitment.

Crew-Cuts

When Ray came into town, he would call or write to ask if I wanted to go to dinner. He, John, and I went back stage at the Ed Sullivan Show to see friends of theirs who were on the show. That was exciting. We would sometimes just go to lunch if they were appearing somewhere nearby.

We never spoke of Rudi. We talked about what Ray might buy P.K. for a birthday or Christmas gift. They were planning to marry, as soon as she set a date. I was wondering how I would handle that wedding. I would be a bridesmaid and Lou was an invited guest, if I wanted him to be. Oh well, I told Ann; I'll worry about that when the time draws near.

I took a six-week home decorating course at one of the furniture stores in the city. One doctor I dated was such a Rangers hockey fan, I asked him to explain the game. I had never been to a game. He was very happy to explain it, thought I was the perfect date, and took me for a bite to eat and to the game. As rough as the game was, I did like hockey, but also wanted to do other things.

I went to the theater as often as I could afford it and when a date asked if I would like to see a show, my answer was always yes.

The Fall of 1957: Moving

I decided to go to New York Hospital (Cornell Medical Center) to work. It was very big compared to Doctors Hospital. I worked some private duty, then went on to work on the 16th floor, which was a private floor and very beautiful. Along with the private rooms, it had a few suites that looked like hotel suites.

It was fun working there, and I made a lot of new friends. We took golf lessons, and went out to shows and dinner every week. I also took riding lessons.

Ann and I moved into a hotel/apartment on Riverside Drive in the 80's, and we each got our own efficiency apartments. We had maid service and message service at the desk, and a coffee shop on the first floor. I loved it.

My parents had now moved to Ohio to be near the rest of the family. I flew home for a weekend to see the new house. A week or two after I returned, Ann said, "You had a phone call late one night. I told them you were away with your fiancé."

I said "Who was it, and what fiancé?"

She said "Rudi. You are doing well without him, you've moved on."

"You had no right to do that," I said. That prompted me to get my own apartment, although we remained close friends.

I never called back. Soon after, I learned he had married again.

Chapter Twelve

FRANK

CHAPTER 12: FRANK

May 1958: Cornell Medical Center, New York City

I had to rush down to the pharmacy to get a medication for a new patient. I turned quickly, almost bumping into a resident, or was he an intern? They all wore the same white uniform; mock turtle neck top, pearl buttons on the one shoulder, white pants and bucks, sometimes a short lab jacket, stethoscope in the pocket. They really looked like doctors. "Hi," he said, "in a hurry?"

I smiled and said, "Yes, I am," and kept going.

A week or so later, some nurses who lived in Queens in a very big apartment invited my former roommate and me to a party on a Saturday night. If we knew any fellows, they said to bring them along.

We just happened to have four cute fellows living on our floor. They were out of college about a year and were starting in the stock market. The company set them up in an apartment during their training. We were just friends going to movies, biking or walking in Central Park, sharing some dinners together. I asked them to the party, and got four yeses.

The six of us walked into the party. Standing in front of the living room fireplace was the resident from the pharmacy, surrounded by a few girls I didn't know. I walked over to him and said "Hi, are you in a hurry?"

"No, not at all. I'm Frank."

"I'm Plus." For once, I'd met someone who didn't ask me to explain the name.

"Can I get you a drink?"

My usual answer; "Whatever you have would be fine."

As he returned, the other girls had moved on. He asked if one of the four escorts was a boyfriend. No, just friends.

"Would you like to sit over there on the couch?" Yes, I would. We monopolized the couch for over two hours, talking. At 11:30 P.M., the resident that came with him thought they should get going since he was going on call in the morning at 6:00.

We planned to meet at 6:00 A.M. Mass, which started a little earlier so that the hospital personnel from across the street could get there, have breakfast, and still get to work on time. Frank told me that he had seen me at church a few times.

When my wakeup call came that morning at 4:30, I turned over and didn't wake up until 6:20. Oh, my God, I was going to be late! I was in charge that day and, I knew, short of help.

I brushed my teeth, threw water on my face, and quickly dressed, then brushed my long hair, grabbed my purse and ran out the door. I jumped in front of a passing cab; maybe it was the white uniform, shoes, and stockings that prevented him from running me down. I don't know if he came to a full stop before I jumped in. I lived on the West Side, 86th and Riverside, and the hospital was in the 60's on the East Side. In the cab, I put on mascara and lipstick. I was ready. I arrived on my floor at 6:55 A.M., pushed my hair under my cap, and grabbed a cup of coffee from the patients' breakfast cart. The night nurse was happy to see me, even if I was ten minutes late.

It was a morning from Hell, starting at 9:30 when I had a serious emergency. The patient was hemorrhaging so badly, and the room quickly filled with interns and residents, doing a cut down (all her veins had collapsed) to start blood and IV's, O2, giving meds, trying to get pressure. After about twenty minutes that seemed like an hour, she was back. I let everyone leave except for one nurse, and I rushed out of the room. Blood on the side of my uniform, and my hair starting to fall out of my cap, I was quite a sight.

Standing next to the door, leaning against the wall was Frank. He said, "I was there. Where were you? Never mind, you don't have to answer." I was thinking he's pretty cute and I just blew it. He said, "How about dinner tonight?" It took me a few seconds to answer yes. "I'll pick you at 7:00," he said, and turned and walked away.

"Hey, you don't know where I live."

"I'll find you," was his answer as he kept walking.

At 11:30 A.M., the desk called me on the intercom, "Miss Conteen, you have a call."

"Hello?"

"I'm sure you are too busy to have lunch," he said.

"That's true," I replied.

"Call me when you get off, and I'll drive you home. Then I'll know exactly where to pick you up tonight."

At 4:30, we met in the E.R. and walked across the street to the garage. We walked up flights of stairs, then kept walking and talking across the longest floor. I was thinking, does he really have a car? Then he stopped at a white Austin Healey sports car, with its top down. I guess he does have a car.

We went to dinner at a little neighborhood restaurant (yes, there are neighborhoods in Manhattan). After dinner, we made a date to meet in the hospital dining room at 6:20 the next morning for breakfast. This time, I was there early.

For the next six weeks, we met for many breakfasts, lunches and, when our schedules were in sync, we went for walks along the East River. We had dinner together every night. We both loved Broadway plays and saw every show there was to see, loved baseball, and took the subway to watch the Yankees. Did I like jazz, Billy Taylor, Dave Brubeck? It was O.K. I really didn't, and when I finally admitted that I didn't, we compromised. I would occasionally go to hear jazz, and he would go with me to an opera. Movies, yes, museums, great, and we both loved to dance.

The interns and residents lived on the 18th floor of the hospital. The evenings Frank was on call, we hung out in the call lounge watching some T.V., sometimes reading medical journals. If there was something I didn't understand, he could always explain it. He made a wonderful teacher.

We ate dinner in the hospital dining room, or at the soda fountain bar. The food was very good at this hospital. If he got called, I would read until he came back, or talk with the other on-call guys. There were very few females in medicine in 1958. Sometimes, someone would cover for a half hour or hour, and we would take a walk along the East River, even in the rain. I would put on a scrub suit and just walk.

It was our fourth week dating, and I knew we were getting serious. He took me to a very expensive restaurant for dinner one Saturday night. I thought that it was probably time to tell him about Miss Uniontown, The Crew-Cuts, my engagement, how it ended, and my second engagement. That was a lot to tell someone in one evening. I already knew his life story.

As the coffee was being poured, I told him I wanted to tell him about a past engagement. When I finished, I said that he could ask me anything he wanted to, and I would answer all questions – but after that, he had to promise never to speak of it again. He promised.

At the end of my story he asked one question, "Are you still in love with Rudi?" "No, but that time will always be a part of my life." He accepted that.

July 2nd, 1958, I was going to Ohio to be a bridesmaid at my friend P.K.'s big, big wedding. As it turned out, she wasn't marrying Ray. Frank drove me to the airport and said, "Have a good time, but don't meet anyone!" He would be leaving for a Surgical Residency in Milwaukee on July 13th.

The wedding and the bride were so beautiful, even though it was one of the hottest weekends I could remember. A heat wave had hit, and the morning of the wedding the thermometer was climbing to 100 degrees. No air conditioning in the church, which was packed with hundreds of people, then a late wedding breakfast for at least two hundred people. We took lots of pictures outside. We went back to the bride's house, took baths with ice cubes in the water, but didn't dare get our hair wet.

The reception for five hundred people started at six that evening. The bridal party stood in the reception line, except for our escorts who kept dropping in and out, until the end. It was a fabulous time, and the couple themselves were having such a great time that we couldn't get them to leave. Etiquette required the bridal party to stay until they left and we threw rice and confetti, and that finally happened at 12:30.

I got back to my parents' house in Elyria, and fell into bed about 2:30 A.M. Five hours later, I was up and off to church, then to a family party so I could visit with everyone. The next morning, we were off to a hospital to visit a sick relative, getting back in time to leave for the airport.

When I met Frank, he was a radiology resident. I really didn't fit into the plans he had at the time for his future. He had four more years of surgical residency. He'd thought that, after that, he'd make a decision as to where he wanted to start his practice, then settle down and think about marriage.

When I got back, I don't think I had slept twenty-four hours in five days. I did sleep on the plane, and when I got off, Frank was waiting for me at the gate. "I don't have to ask if you had a good time, it shows."

"Yes, I did."

"You know," he said, "I can't leave you in this city alone. I love you, will you marry me?"

It took me only a second to say "yes."

After we kissed, people staring at us and smiling, he said, "I'll never let you down."

I knew he meant it! These last three years, I'd looked fine on the outside, but on the inside I was broken. I couldn't love because I couldn't trust, and now, with him, I was healed. He was my "Knight in Shining Armor."

The Handsome Doctor, Frank Hall.

The Love of My Life.

July 1958: The Proposal

The next day, I called my mother and told her that I was getting married on September 6th, and would she please see if the church was available, along with the priest I liked. I would call the Greystone Hotel to book the reception as soon as I had the church date. I really wanted a small wedding with all the trimmings, but I did emphasize "small." The last wedding I'd been in had overwhelmed me, and I hadn't even been the bride.

Frank and I only had one more week together before he left for Milwaukee with another resident friend, in his small white Austin Healy Sports car. Their first stop was Elyria, Ohio, to meet and have dinner with my folks, his new in-laws-to-be. I felt sorry I couldn't be with him.

Dinner was a success. I called while they were still there.

Beginning of August 1958

Frank had made a trip to Elyria, and I hadn't seen him for three weeks. He looked great. We had to get the license and blood tests, and also meet with the priest. My mother still looked at Frank with a skeptical eye. She gave a party so that the rest of our family could meet him. He would not be returning until two days before the wedding. I felt sorry for him, knowing that he'd be placed under a microscope. He carried it off brilliantly, with all the confidence in the world. Thanks to his smile and sense of humor, my extended family warmed up to him immediately, just as I had.

After three years, I was still keeping a low profile, so when his parents asked for a picture to put in the New York and Meriden, Connecticut papers, I politely declined, saying I was so busy planning everything. "In two months time, let's just put in a wedding picture." They had no idea about the 1955 fiasco. After a few requests, they dropped it. My soon-to-be sister-in-law Nancy announced that she and her fiancé, Ron, would be getting married in November (instead of June). Great, that took the pressure off of me.

Frank had picked out two small apartments near the hospital, so I went back to Milwaukee with him to give my OK to one of them, and buy a few things to enhance it since it was already furnished. I thought it was great and convenient. Having only one car, we could easily walk to the hospital. I had an interview there, and would be working in Pediatrics and Newborn Premature Nursery.

He had friends there, since he had done his internship at Milwaukee County General Hospital. I told Frank about my first time in Milwaukee while we were driving there. It is sometimes so strange how things happen. While we were in Milwaukee, Frank was also having me meet his friends. His big surprise was taking me out to, as he put it, "one of the best very New York-style clubs" on Saturday night to celebrate. The club was Fazio's. Another lovely place was chosen for the occasion. Late Sunday afternoon, I flew back home.

Two Days until the Wedding

The wedding day was approaching fast. September 4th was very busy; bridesmaids arriving and going for their fittings, Frank's family flying in, and also some arriving by car. But the best part of the day was the groom flying in at 6 P.M. The Cleveland Airport was just forty minutes away, but the drive seemed so long. This time, I was waiting at the gate.

I saw his big smile, and asked, "Are you in a hurry?"

"No, I'm not," he said,

"Then how about getting married in about forty hours?" I said.

He said, "I would love that," and he kissed me.

The rehearsal party was as festive as a wedding, with one of Frank's aunts playing the piano, and everyone dancing and singing until after 11.

Wedding Day

We talked about getting married in Uniontown, or Connecticut was an option, but we decided that Elyria, Ohio would be the easiest for my parents and family.

I was adamant that the wedding guests would be only family and very close friends, no more than 100. St. Mary's was a beautiful, small, very old, Catholic church.

The wedding party would be twelve, plus the two of us. My bouquet would not be the traditional white; I wanted cascading long-stemmed, deep red, American Beauty roses, with sparkly white satin ribbon. I decided not to tell my grandmother ahead of time – she would not like breaking tradition – but I knew she would love it when she saw it, and she did.

My gown was oyster white silk peau de soie, with a basque waist, and a scalloped scoop neckline, trimmed with pastel sequins. Long sleeves, full long skirt, with chapel train. Long chapel-length veil of silk illusion, held by a French tiara of filigree, trimmed with rhinestones and pearls; somewhat conservative, but beautiful.

The reception was a lovely luncheon. Partying and dinner continued at my parents' home, but we flew off at 5 P.M. It was a beautiful day.

Elyria, Ohio Is Scene Of Lovely Summer Ceremony; To Reside In Milwaukee

The Evening Standard

Uniontown, Pa. SEP 12 1958

Prominent among the late summer weddings was that of Placeda Dee Conteen, daughter of Mr. and Mrs. Charles D'Zamba, 314 Seventh St., Elyria, Ohio, and Dr. Francis M. Hall Jr., son of Mr. and Mrs. Francis M. Hall, 51 Cottage St., Meriden, Conn., which was solemnized on Saturday morning, Sept. 6, in St. Mary's Church, Elyria, at 10:30.

The Rev. James McCann officiated at the lovely nuptial High Mass before an altar banked with gladiolas and pompons.

Escorted to the altar by her step-father, the bride appeared in an oyster white floor-length gown of silk peau de soie designed with basque waist, scalloped scoop neckline trimmed with sequins, and long tapered sleeves that were pointed at the wrists. The full skirt terminated in a chapel train. Her long chapel-length veil of silk illusion was held by a French tiara crown of filegose trimmed with rhinestones and pearl. She carried a cascade bouquet of American Beauty roses with ivy trim and white satin streamers.

Mrs. Ceatta Plickey, Cleveland, Ohio, was her cousin's matron of honor. She appeared in a cobalt blue velvet sheath designed with scoop neckline, short sleeves and nylon satin bow in back. Completing her ensemble was a cascade bouquet of Pinocchio pompons with blue center and silver foliage and tricotine streamers.

Bridesmaids were Nancy Hall, sister of the bridegroom; Ann Ruby, New York; Mrs. Les Riemenschneider, Pittsburgh, and Mrs. Pat Wendling, Cleveland. Their gowns were styled identically to the one worn by the matron of honor. Each carried a cascade bouquet of white Pinocchio pompons.

Serving as her cousin's flower girl was Mary Frances Cunningham of Lorain, Ohio. She was attired similarly to the other attendants and carried a basket arrangements of blue and white Pinocchio pompons with blue satin streamers.

Britt Hall of Meriden, Conn., was his brother's best man. Ushering were E. J. O'Brien, Meriden; Ronald Duncan, Granby, Conn.; Dr. Gaspar Encarnucion, Puerto Rico, and Dr. Anthony Cairo, Milwaukee, Wis.

Steve Meballic, cousin of the bride, was the page.

For her daughter's wedding Mrs. D'Zamba chose a light blue lace sheath with matching accessories and a corsage of white roses with blue forget-me-nots with silver trim. Mrs. Hall, mother of the bridegroom, chose a blue and green pure silk print sheath with matching accessories and a corsage of white roses and stephanotis.

Following the ceremony a reception for 75 guests was held at the Greystone Hotel.

When the couple left for a wedding trip of unrevealed destination, the bride was wearing an electric blue sheath, ranch mink furs, blue and green satin hat, white gloves and black accessories. At the conclusion of the trip they will reside in Milwaukee, Wis.

The new Mrs. Hall is a 1951 graduate of North Union Twp. High School. She graduated from Allegheny General Hospital School of Nursing in 1954 and is a former winner of the Miss Uniontown contest.

Dr. Hall received his B.S. degree from St. Lawrence University, Canton, N. Y., in 1950. He received his M.S. degree in 1952 from Syracuse University, Syracuse, N. Y., and his M.D. degree from New York Medical School. He did his internship at Milwaukee County General Hospital and was a resident doctor at Cornell Medical Center. He is presently a resident doctor at Milwaukee County General Hospital.

MRS. FRANCIS M. HALL JR.
—Svat Studio

September 1958: Milwaukee

Frank had only five days off, since this was very early in his residency, and in another five days I would be returning to work.

At times, we could manage to have breakfast or lunch together, but not like we had when we were at Cornell Medical Center. Frank's schedule was very busy.

From the time I graduated, I could usually name where I wanted to work and when. It was different here; they needed me in the Pediatric and Preemie Nursery and that is where I worked my three shifts. It wasn't easy trying to get the same weekends off as Frank's; many times, we weren't even off on the same nights. Weekends, he would leave Saturday mornings and not return until Monday evening.

I decided to take a modeling course, to pass the time when Frank was gone, and also to help me to make friends. Although I had modeled as a teen, this seemed like the best way to get some modeling work here. It was fun, and I did two local T.V. shows and a couple other store shows, but my nursing schedule came first.

One weekend in October, Frank and five other residents were planning on the six couples going to the Notre Dame football game in South Bend, Indiana. On Friday afternoon, I came home from work with a temperature of 100 degrees and nausea. I went to bed and slept for a couple of hours. When Frank got home, he found a sick wife. I was now starting to vomit every couple of hours.

Saturday morning, I was so weak from being up all night that I knew I would not be able to go to the big game. Frank got me some medicine for the flu, and watched the game at the call room at the hospital.

Monday morning, I was still so sick that I couldn't go to work. Frank reluctantly left me at 6 A.M. At 6:45, the doctor friend he'd sent over to check on me arrived. Dr. Dave listened to my symptoms, took my pressure, and said, "You're pregnant, probably three weeks." He gave me a prescription for nausea and his office number to call for an appointment. Thirty-six hours later, I was back to work.

By November, I was still feeling quite ill, but I was able to work. The doctors wanted to admit me to the hospital so I could receive intravenous fluids for a few days. I wouldn't do that because we did not want the hospital to know that I was pregnant. The work policy at this time was you had to resign your position at five months. We really couldn't afford to do that. I did resign in my seventh month, which they thought was my fifth.

Also in November, we flew to Connecticut. Frank was an usher in his sister Nancy's wedding.

Christmas, we both worked, but we had dinner at our friends', Carol and Don. No family, but some very good friends and a very nice Christmas.

At the end of my sixth month, I was feeling somewhat better and started to gain weight. We were now looking for a larger apartment. We moved into a five-room, first floor apartment in the same little town of Wauwatosa.

June 1959: Suzie

My mother arrived early in June to await the arrival of her first grandchild. Two weeks later, on a bright sunny Sunday morning, I woke Frank at 6 in the morning to say I was in labor. His "Are you sure?" was answered with a labor pain that doubled me over, and he moved very quickly. We woke Mom to say we were leaving. I had been awake for the last six and a half hours.

We arrived at the hospital at 6:25, and Susan (Suzie) Veronica Hall was born at 7:55A.M. Veronica was my mother's name. In September, we went home to Ohio and Connecticut to introduce the latest member of the family.

Frank and I were now sure we would not be setting up practice in Milwaukee. We wanted our children to grow up around family. Frank thought it would be beneficial to finish his residency where he would be starting his practice. He interviewed at Allegheny General, Elyria, and in Hartford, and was accepted by all. Now we had to make the big decision, and Connecticut was it.

New Year's Eve Day Morning, 1959

6 A.M. Frank kisses me goodbye, "I will call later – love you, girls."

"We love you, too."

My folks came for Christmas, so Frank took that holiday off. It was an easy exchange because the single guys wanted to celebrate New Year's Eve.

Frank called when Suzie and I were having dinner. He had just finished a surgery, and the E.R. was very busy, but he promised that he would call before midnight.

At 7:30, I put Suzie to bed and sat down to read and make a few New Year's phone calls. The phone rang; it was Frank.

"I just called to say I love you," he said, "I'm going into surgery, a ruptured spleen on a young boy, car accident. I might miss calling at midnight so, honey, Happy New Year. I will hopefully be home tomorrow about noon, and we will celebrate the New Year then."

I sat and reviewed my 50's. My decade was over, but so much had happened. Love, lots of love, which made the sad times bearable. They say things happen for a reason, and I hadn't always believed that. But I was certainly beginning to. Our plans for the new decade were made. As of July 1, 1960, Suzie and I would be leaving to spend the 4th of July with family in Ohio, then flying to Connecticut where Daddy would meet us at our new apartment, in a beautiful town called West Hartford, about twelve minutes from St. Francis Hospital and Medical Center in Hartford, the largest Catholic Hospital in New England, where Frank would finish his surgical residency in two years. As soon as I found the proper babysitter, I would be working there.

At 11:45 P.M., I turned the TV on to watch the New Year and the new decade ushered in. I sat for a moment, reflecting on all that happened. If I could have looked into a crystal ball that New Year's Day 1950, I could not have begun to imagine so much could have happened in ten years.

At 11:55 P.M. the phone rang. "Hi, honey, I just finished surgery. I had to call and wish you happy New Year again, and tell you this year has been a ball. I love you."

"I hope you get some sleep. See you in twelve hours. I love you. Happy New Year."

In Closing

My beloved husband, Frank M. Hall, M.D., died June 8th, 2005 at home after a courageous three-year battle with melanoma. Truly, he was my Knight in Shining Armor.

A year and a half later, I learned of the death of Rudi.

Rudi Maugeri died May 7th, 2004, almost 50 years to the day that I had met him, (May 4, 1954) of pancreatic cancer. He had resided in Las Vegas with his third wife at the time.

John Perkins and his lovely wife, Gilda, live in Slidell, Louisiana. He is the music director of St. Margaret Mary Church, has remained active in music, and is a Commissioner on the city's arts council.

Ray Perkins is retired and lives in Redmond, Washington with his wife, Dorrie.

Patrick Barrett and his terrific wife, Ellen, are living in Tuckerton, New Jersey. Pat is still writing music. They remain my dear friends.

What a journey we all had in the 50's.

No Regrets? No Regrets!

Printed in the USA
CPSIA information can be obtained
at www.ICGtesting.com
JSHW012018140824
68134JS00033B/2764